OPERATION *CHARIOT*
THE ST NAZAIRE RAID, 1942

CASEMATE | ILLUSTRATED

◖ CASEMATE | ILLUSTRATED

OPERATION CHARIOT

THE ST NAZAIRE RAID, 1942

JEAN-CHARLES STASI

CASEMATE | ILLUSTRATED

To Major-General Corran Purdon, to Stephen Barney, to Bill "Tiger" Watson, James Dorrian, Hubert Chemereau, to the Commando Veterans' Association, to the "Mémoire et savoir nazairiens" association, to the St Nazaire Municipal Archives and Ecomuseum; to Laurent Lemel, Gérard Cerizier, Paul Gros, Thierry Vallet and the whole team at Heimdal.— Jean-Charles Stasi

CIS0013

Print Edition: ISBN 978-1-61200-7298
Digital Edition: ISBN 978-1-61200-7304

This book is published in cooperation with and under license from Heimdal. Originally published in French as *Saint-Nazaire, 28 mars 1942 "Chariot," Le plus grand raid commando de la seconde guerre mondiale* © Heimdal 2018

Typeset, design and additional material © Casemate Publishers 2019
Translation by Hannah McAdams
Design by Battlefield Design
Color artwork by Jean Restayn
Infographics by Paul Gros
Color profiles by Thierry Vallet
Additional text by Chris Cocks
Original cartography by Sandra Gosselin
Printed and bound by Megaprint, Turkey.

CASEMATE PUBLISHERS (US)
Telephone (610) 853-9131
Fax (610) 853-9146
Email: casemate@casematepublishers.com
www.casematepublishers.com

CASEMATE PUBLISHERS (UK)
Telephone (01865) 241249
Fax (01865) 794449
Email: casemate-uk@casematepublishers.co.uk
www.casematepublishers.co.uk

Title page: One of the many Flak pieces protecting the port of St Nazaire, positioned on the roof of the cold-storage warehouse. (St Nazaire Ecomuseum)
Contents page: After crossing under the bascule bridge at the New Entrance, Lieutenant-Commander Erich Topp's *U-552* (Topp is on the turret, in the center) enters the old basin. With several kills to his name, Topp was certainly the most photographed of the U-boat captains at St Nazaire. His motto was "The red devil, come to bring fire to England." (Unknown/ECPAD/Defense)
Map: The commando raid (March 28, 1942)

Note: vehicle illustrations and profiles are not to scale.

Contents

| Timeline of Events

Between May 26 and June 4, 1940, 338,000 Allied troops—predominantly British Expeditionary Force, and remnants from the French and Polish armies—were evacuated from the beaches of Dunkirk. Britain now truly stood alone against the might of the Third Reich. On May 27, 1941, the German battleship *Bismarck* was sunk by the Royal Navy in the running battle of the Denmark Strait, but not before HMS *Hood*, the pride of the Royal Navy, was dispatched to the seabed. On June 17, 1940 RMS *Lancastria*, evacuating Allied troops during the fall of France, was sunk by the Luftwaffe in St Nazaire harbor with the loss of up to 5,800 lives. It was the worst maritime disaster of British history. The only way the British, their backs desperately to the wall, knew how to strike back was through commando raids against German facilities on the European continent. Pinpricks at first, the raids were soon to grow in scale and intensity …

June 24/25, 1940 Operation *Collar*, first-ever British commando raid (by No.11 Independent Company) on Boulogne

July 17, 1940 Admiral of the Fleet Roger Keyes becomes first director of new Combined Operations HQ

March 4, 1941 Operation *Claymore*, successful large-scale British commando raid on Norwegian Lofoten Islands; German encryption codes captured

October 28, 1941 Admiral of the Fleet Lord Louis Mountbatten appointed director of Combined Operations HQ. British Naval Intelligence proposes raid against St Nazaire

December 27, 1941 Operation *Archery*, the Maloy Raid, successful commando raid against German positions on the island of Vaagso, Norway

HMS *Tynedale* was one of the flotilla's two escorts. This *Hunt*-class destroyer was launched in 1940. On December 15, 1941, it was transferred to the Devonport-based 15th Destroyer Flotilla at Plymouth. Damaged in the Mediterranean in 1943, it was sunk on December 12 of the same year by *U-593* off Jijel, Algeria. Ironically, *U-593* was the same German submarine the *Tynedale* encountered on the morning of March 27, 1942, on its way to St Nazaire. (Imperial War Museum)

Aerial photo of St Nazaire, taken by a Royal Air Force reconnaissance aircraft. (The National Archives)

January 16, 1942
German battleship *Tirpitz* departs Wilhelmshaven to lie in wait in the Norwegian fjords

March 26, 1942
Chariot strike force convoy departs Falmouth, Cornwall, at 1400, for St Nazaire, France

March 27, 1942
Convoy arrives off Loire estuary; at 2330, RAF commences bombing run over St Nazaire

March 29, 1942
Last surviving MLs reach England

JANUARY 1942   FEBRUARY 1942   MARCH 1942

February 1, 1942
Commando–Royal Navy raid on St Nazaire confirmed; planning for Operation *Chariot* begins

March 28, 1942

HMS *Campbeltown* rams dock gates at 0134; battle of St Nazaire proper begins

Commando demolition teams destroy major port installations

At dawn Lt-Col Newman orders general withdrawal

At 0530 ML 14 in epic battle with German torpedo boat *Jaguar*

By mid-morning all commandos at the port, bar 5, are captured

Campbeltown charges detonate at noon, killing 200–400 Germans

March 30, 1942
2 x delayed-action torpedoes explode, preempting German reprisals against local residents

7

The British Face the Threat of the *Tirpitz*

In early 1942, the prospect of the formidable German battleship, the *Tirpitz*, patrolling the Atlantic was a horrifying prospect for the Allied convoys supplying Britain. British Prime Minister Winston Churchill now had just one thing on his mind: neutralizing this giant of the seas.

Since the war began, the Kriegsmarine—the German navy—had been sowing terror in the Atlantic. German submarines—*Unterseeboote*, or U-boats—were relentlessly attacking supply convoys bound for Great Britain, sinking an increased tonnage of shipping every month. The U-boat torpedoes hit their mark almost every time, eviscerating the cumbersome cargo vessels, inadequately protected by their escorts that lacked effective detection methods.

British Prime Minister Winston Churchill was only too aware that his country would find itself exsanguinated if the situation persisted. He was obsessed with the battle of the Atlantic because he well knew that the future of the conflict rested on its outcome. With German troops occupying most of Western Europe, with the exception of Switzerland, Sweden and the Iberian Peninsula, how could the United Kingdom continue fighting if it found itself starved of ore, fuel, food, weapons, and munitions?

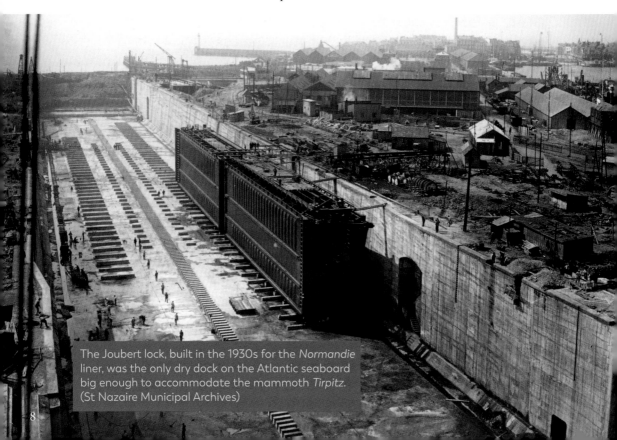

The Joubert lock, built in the 1930s for the *Normandie* liner, was the only dry dock on the Atlantic seaboard big enough to accommodate the mammoth *Tirpitz*. (St Nazaire Municipal Archives)

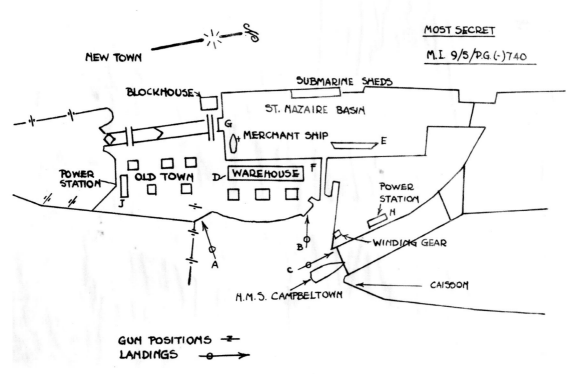

NEW TOWN

BLOCKHOUSE

SUBMARINE SHEDS

ST. NAZAIRE BASIN

G

MERCHANT SHIP

E

POWER STATION

OLD TOWN

D

WAREHOUSE

F

J

POWER STATION

H

B

WINDING GEAR

A

C

CAISSON

H.M.S. CAMPBELTOWN

GUN POSITIONS

LANDINGS

A "Most Secret" British sketch of the port facilities at St Nazaire. At the bottom right is the HMS *Campbeltown*, about to pass through the Joubert caisson.
(The National Archives)

In early 1942, a new threat joined the U-boat wolf packs. On January 16, the *Tirpitz* left its home port of Wilhelmshaven to lie in wait in the Norwegian fjords: the Nazi battleship was thus ideally placed to attack Arctic convoys supporting the Soviet war effort, as well as the cumbersome convoys of merchant ships that, farther south, were making their way towards England.

Sister ship to the *Bismarck* that was sunk by the Royal Navy on May 27, 1941, three days after it had sent the pride of the Royal Navy, the battlecruiser HMS *Hood* and 1,400 of its crew to the bottom of the Atlantic, the *Tirpitz* represented a greater threat than dozens of submarines combined. Over 250 meters long, with a crew of 2,600, it was armed with 60 guns, of which eight were 38cm caliber, not to mention its eight torpedo launch tubes, four Arado 196 floatplanes and armor plating of unparalleled thickness.

Churchill's worries were thus entirely justified, especially as the *Tirpitz* could easily be joined in Norway by the cruisers *Scharnhorst*, *Gneisenau* and *Prinz Eugen*, which were waiting in Brest, ready to take to the seas and force the British blockade in the Pas de Calais.

In a note dated January 25 and addressed to the Chiefs of Staff of the British armed forces, the British prime minister emphasized the magnitude of the threat the arrival of the *Tirpitz* posed, not only to their own country, the United Kingdom, but to the entire Allied war effort: "The destruction or even crippling of this ship is the greatest event at sea at the present time. No other target is comparable to it."

With the gravity of the situation very clear, the next step was to establish how to neutralize the *Tirpitz*. The first and obvious solution that came to mind was to sink it. The

The Joubert lock today. The pumping station, one of the British commandos' objectives, is visible on the right. (J.-C. Stasi)

best way to accomplish this would be to lure— or force—it to leave its Norwegian haven, but following the *Hood* tragedy, the British knew only too well the risk and cost of such an offensive action. Certainly, the *Bismarck* now lay in some five kilometers of water, 659 kilometers northwest of Brest, but putting it there had cost the Home Fleet its best ship and 1,415 seamen, provoking a national tragedy and striking a terrible blow to the morale of the British people.

So, instead of attacking the *Tirpitz* directly, how could they prevent it from making mischief? The Admiralty was not going to wait for Hitler to order the ship out of its Norwegian berth. The solution quickly manifested itself: to stop the *Tirpitz* from appearing in the Atlantic, they had to remove every opportunity for repair or maintenance along the entire coastline controlled by the forces of the Third Reich. Luckily for the British, outside of Germany, there was only one dry dock that was large enough to house the 250-meter, 50,000-ton behemoth: the Joubert lock at St Nazaire. At 350 meters in length, it was 100 meters longer than the one at the Kriegsmarine's flagship port of Wilhelmshaven. In addition, the lock's 50-meter breadth and 15-meter height meant it could accommodate vessels of up to 85,000 tons.

In addition to its use as a dry dock, the Joubert lock also operated as a lock between the Loire estuary and the Penhoët basin, which served as the gateway to the shipyards of the same name. Indeed, it had at each end a gigantic rolling door, or gates, made of solid steel. Being 52 meters long and 11 meters deep, these two doors operated by sliding laterally, open and closed, on rolling trolleys, rather than opening and closing like a set of double doors as in regular locks.

Its size, its versatility, and the modernity of its equipment made this unique dock the ideal refuge for a ship the size of the *Tirpitz*. Indeed, it was toward St Nazaire that the *Bismarck* was heading when it was torpedoed by the Royal Navy on the morning of May 27,

1941. The British had nicknamed it the "Normandie Dock," as the *Normandie*, the largest liner of the time at 313 meters, had been berthed there from the early 1930s. The *Normandie* was launched in October 1932 and entered service in May 1935.

Beyond its strategic value, St Nazaire gave the British an opportunity for revenge. In mid-June 1940, following the evacuations at Dunkirk, some 40,000 men from the British Expeditionary Force had converged on the port to depart for England. Among them were also elements of the Polish and Czech armies. On the 17th, the day that Marshal Pétain requested Germany open peace negotiations with France, the Luftwaffe attacked the Cunard White Star liner RMS *Lancastria* at St Nazaire, which was carrying both military personnel and civilians. Hit by several bombs, the 13,000-ton ship sank within minutes, causing the deaths of between 3,000 and 5,800 people. It was Britain's largest maritime disaster in history, but was never publicized as survivors were expressly forbidden from talking about it.

The possibility of an offensive action against St Nazaire was initially mooted in August 1941. Encouraged by the success of the earlier raid on Norway—Operation *Claymore*, a British commando raid on the Lofoten Islands in March 1941—the Admiralty had asked the Royal Navy to consider the possibility of a joint attack with Combined Operations Headquarters, a department of the British War Office set up in the immediate aftermath of the evacuation of Dunkirk to harass the Germans in Europe through combined naval and commando raids. As well as the Joubert lock, it also sought to attack the submarine base, which was effectively indestructible by aircraft due to the thickness of the reinforced concrete slabs of its roof.

Aerial view of the *Normandie* liner in the Joubert lock. (The National Archives)

The *Normandie* in the Joubert lock. (St Nazaire Municipal Archives)

One of the gates of the Joubert lock. The people in the foreground give you an idea of the scale of the dock (The National Archives)

Admiral of the Fleet Sir Charles Forbes, charged with working out this double-objective, made his report in the fall of 1942. His conclusions could not have been clearer: given the means and manpower currently available to the British armed forces, he deemed the mission impracticable, and the obstacles facing them insurmountable. Indeed, how were they to retain the element of surprise, indispensable in such an operation, when they had to travel all the way from the south of England to St Nazaire, a distance of 700 kilometers, or 435 miles, without being spotted? And how were they to navigate the shoals that made the estuary such a dangerous place for shipping? And how on earth were they going to transport enough troops—they would need at least 300—complete with their equipment, as well as the demolition teams?

In short, there were more cons than pros, and the project was abandoned. But by the close of 1941, the threat of *Tirpitz* once again loomed large, and brought the issue back to the fore. By the beginning of 1942, Churchill was confident that he could rely on a man whom he saw as both dynamic and imaginative: Vice-Admiral Louis Mountbatten, who, at 41 years of age, had been appointed by the prime minister as Chief of Combined Operations in October 1941. Hailing from the highest ranks of British nobility, cousin of King George VI, and nephew of Tsarina Alexandra, Louis Mountbatten—"Dicky"—was a charismatic and celebrated senior naval officer, boasting an adequate intelligence.

Provided to British intelligence by the French Resistance, this sketch of the technical installations of the pump station proved invaluable for the preparation and training of the demolition teams. (The National Archives)

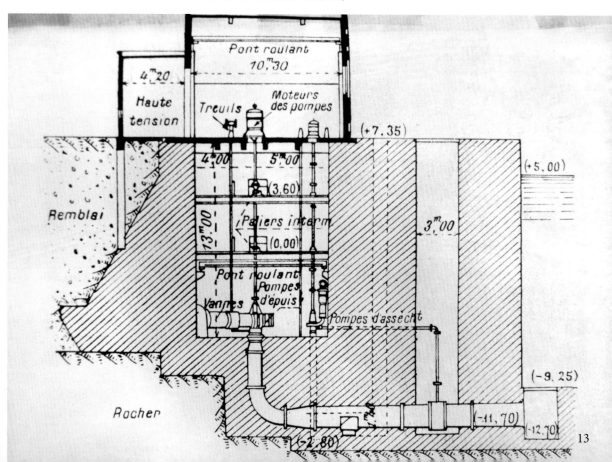

In Profile:
The *Tirpitz*

Shortly after he took over the reins of Combined Operations, he conceived and launched a commando raid on Norway: Operation *Archery*, or the Maloy Raid as it came to be known, was a Combined Operations raid against German positions on the Norwegian island of Vaagso, on December 27, 1941. The operation was wildly successful, allowing the British commandos to capture the German naval encryption system not only for Kriegsmarine vessels based in Norway, but also those in France.

In true "Dicky" fashion, Mountbatten dived headlong into the St Nazaire project with all his customary initiative, effectively assisted by a staff of talented and enthusiastic officers. Based at Richmond Terrace, between Whitehall and the Thames River, Mountbatten's team worked round the clock, making rapid and significant progress in the planning of the operation.

While scouring the nautical charts of the St Nazaire sector, Vice-Admiral John Hughes-Hallett, a naval adviser, made an important discovery that could ostensibly reinforce the feasibility of an attack by sea: at spring tide, when the tide was at its highest, it would be just about achievable for shallow-draft boats to traverse the sandbars which, under ordinary conditions, made navigation in the Loire estuary so difficult. Thus, it would be possible to make it to St Nazaire without taking the traditional Charpentiers Channel, which was usually much safer, but directly exposed to German artillery fire.

As for the Marquis de Casa Maury, who was responsible for gathering all the necessary information and detail needed to prepare each raid, he too made a significant breakthrough, having over the past year gathered critical documentation on the St Nazaire objective. In addition to the photos taken by Royal Air Force (RAF) reconnaissance aircraft, he had collated detailed maps, sketches and technical notes not only on the coastal defenses, but also on the port facilities and the submarine base. Some of this information had been provided by the French Resistance. In early 1941, a young St Nazaire local, Hugues Mainguy, met British agents in the *Zone Libre* (free zone) and handed over plans of the base that he had

The battleship *Tirpitz*—sister ship of the *Bismarck* that was sunk by the Royal Navy on May 27, 1941—was launched by Adolf Hitler himself in Wilhelmshaven on April 1, 1939. With a length of 251 meters, a width of 36 meters and a draft of 11 meters, it was the Kriegsmarine's largest warship. In some places, its armor measured a staggering 323mm. It was armed with eight 38cm guns, secondary artillery and an antiaircraft defense system. The 38cm guns were paired in four turrets, named Anton and Bruno in the bow, and Cæsar and Dora in the stern. Secondary artillery consisted of 12 15cm guns in six turrets, and 16 10.5cm guns on dual mounts, plus 16 3.7cm antiaircraft guns and 80 2cm rapid-fire guns. The *Tirpitz* also carried four Arado Ar 196 floatplanes. (Thierry Vallet)

obtained from a local architect who had been drafted by the Todt Organization, the German civil and military engineering organization. The Resistance was also responsible for handing the British another equally valuable document: a highly detailed sketch of the Joubert lock's pump installations, indicating the respective depths of each level.

Combined Operations had one more "secret weapon" at their disposal: a model of the port of St Nazaire, made for them by the modeling division of the RAF's photo-reconnaissance section. In the days and weeks that followed, this faithful reproduction of the future theater of operations—a perimeter around 1.5 kilometers in length and 500 meters wide—proved invaluable, both for those making the plans and those who had to execute them.

Lord Mountbatten, center, flanked by his Combined Operations staff. (The National Archives)

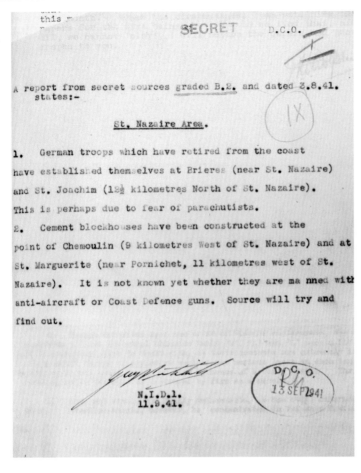

As this classified note from 1941 attests, St Nazaire and its environs, heavily fortified by the Germans, was a major British objective. (The National Archives)

The model showed two piers extending about 400 meters into the estuary, which at that point was about 1.5 kilometers wide. These two piers delimited the outer harbor, at the end of which was the main entrance, also known as the Southern Entrance or *Nouvelle Entrée* (New Entrance). This in turn, through a series of four locks, provided access to the St Nazaire basin, where the submarine base was located. This short "junction" canal passed through a residential area that included the old town, which Nazairians had nicknamed *Petit Maroc* (Little Morocco), characterized by its narrow streets and low houses.

The basin of St Nazaire overlooked the Penhoët basin to the north. It was bordered on the west by the ever-growing naval base and its ancillary buildings; opposite was a large area given over to warehouses and shops, situated between the "Old Mole" jetty (approximately 200 meters long) and the *Vielle Entrée* (Old Entrance), also connected to the basin.

Adjoining the Old Entrance, and oriented largely north–south, the Joubert lock was angled diagonally to the Penhoët basin, with access granted through one of the two enormous caisson doors that the British were so preoccupied with.

The specialists at Combined Operations, however, noted with some relief that the southern entrance to the dock was not protected from a maritime attack by a boom, but by a simple torpedo net stretched across the channel, about 50 meters upstream. Logically, this net would be easier to neutralize than a more solid obstruction.

A detailed examination of photos and other documents provided much information about the giant lock. The rolling steel doors were operated using a powerful system of moveable rack-and-pinion hinges, housed alongside their engines at two operating positions, one at each end. To fulfill its function as a lock, the dock also had a pumping station, the engines of which were at ground level, though the pumps themselves were more than ten meters below.

While Mountbatten and his staff were pleased to find that the pump station and the gate-operating stations were all grouped nicely together on the western quay, their hopes of an easy operation were soon dashed when they realized that it would be impossible to destroy the 10-meter-thick caissons with only the explosives that the commandos could carry. They would have to find another way.

It was the same for the submarine base. With 3.5 meters of solid concrete topping its roof, designed to withstand even the most powerful bombs, it was inconceivable that shipborne demolition crews might succeed where even the RAF would fail. Explosives that could raze St Nazaire to the ground would barely leave a scratch on that mass of reinforced concrete.

But the British were not put off, and reflecting on the problem soon led their strategists to a novel solution. While they could not necessarily destroy the base, they could put it out of action by destroying the lock gates that led to the basin. From the maps, they concluded that there were six lock systems in total serving the basin: two at the Old Entrance, and four at the New Entrance. Including the Joubert lock caissons, this brought the total to eight.

The Combined Operations strategists also discovered the presence of large fuel tanks, buried under concrete and earth at the southern entrance of the Joubert lock. In addition, they drew attention to the warehouse and workshop area, which was where the power plant was located.

In the end, no less than 24 objectives were decided upon: the destruction of the Normandie Dock's two gigantic doors remained the top priority, followed by the neutralization of the six other locks, as well as four bridges, six power stations and six artillery batteries, the latter comprising 13 pieces of varying calibers.

In short, the mission was turning out to be far more ambitious than had originally been envisaged the year before. It followed then, that it would be more difficult to achieve, and would demand a greater price in human life.

The British quickly realized that destroying the submarine base from the air was impossible, due to the thick slabs of reinforced concrete that can still be seen on the facility's roof. (St Nazaire Municipal Archives)

17

This photo shows that the base was built within the city. In the foreground is the wooden scaffolding at the beginning of construction, and in the background are houses on Admiral Courbet Street, destroyed by Allied bombing. (St Nazaire Municipal Archive)

| The Estuary and the Lock

It was going to be a tough mission for the British commandos: because of the submarine base, the Germans had made the port of St Nazaire and the Loire estuary one of the most heavily defended sectors on the Western European coastline.

On June 21, 1940, two days after the newly completed French battleship *Jean Bart* left the Penhoët basin under the cover of darkness, the Germans arrived in St Nazaire. In the fall, they decided to build a submarine base there, with the dual advantage of direct access to the sea and the shelter of the Loire estuary. St Nazaire was to become one of the five bastions of the Kriegsmarine on the Atlantic, along with Brest, Lorient, La Pallice (La Rochelle), and Bordeaux.

The site was handed over to the Todt Organization, and work began in February 1941. The dock where the Compagnie Générale Transatlantique warships had been berthed was subsequently drained. Keen to complete the project as quickly as possible, the Germans halted all other public works in the area, drawing heavily on local and foreign labor. Supporting the 1,500 Todt Organization members were some 3,000 indentured laborers, mostly French, but

Unlike the city itself, which was all but destroyed by Allied bombing, the submarine base withstood raids by both British and American air forces. (St Nazaire Municipal Archives)

This photo of the submarine base roof being reinforced was taken from the terrace of the cold-storage warehouse sometime before March 1942. (St Nazaire Ecomuseum)

A U-boat prepares to enter the submarine base. (St Nazaire Municipal Archives)

also Belgians, North Africans, Italians, Dutch, Czechoslovaks, Russians, and even Spanish Republican refugees dispatched to the Loire-Inferieure by the Vichy government.

In the center of town, not far from the train station, the site was a vast, restless hive of activity. Twenty-four hours a day, in daylight or under spotlight, workers were busy building walls and pouring concrete produced by dozens of cement mixers. A specially developed railway allowed for the continuous flow of sand extracted from the Loire.

On June 30, 1941, Fritz Todt handed the keys to the base over to Admiral Karl Dönitz, U-boat Commander-in-Chief, who had just arrived from his command at Lorient. That same day, *U-303* became the first U-boat to enter the base, its arrival watched by thousands of workers gathered on top of the scaffolding that had yet to be dismantled.

The base continued to ramp up its operations to cope with the intensification of the U-boat campaign. In July 1941, work started on a new series of submarine pens, which were completed in January 1942. This extension allowed the 7th U-boat Flotilla, hailing from Kiel, to be reinforced by the 6th U-boat Flotilla, previously stationed in Danzig. Both units used type VII U-boats, the most widely produced German submarine. The 7th U-boat Flotilla was commanded by Lieutenant-Commander (Korvettenkapitän) Herbert Sohler, and the 6th by Lieutenant-Commander Wilhelm Schulz.

By the end of February 1942, with nine pens already completed, the third stage of expansion was already well underway; the fourth and final stage was carried out between June and December 1943, bringing the final count to 14 submarine pens (eight single repair pens and six with a capacity of two submarines each).

It took nearly 500,000 cubic meters of concrete to build the massive submarine base, which was 300 meters long, 124 meters wide and 18 meters high, occupying nearly 40,000 square meters of ground space.

British air attacks against St Nazaire went back to early 1941, with the bombing campaign increasing incrementally, both in frequency and intensity. But while the RAF caused major damage to the surroundings, it had almost no effect on the submarine base.

Initially constructed to a thickness of 3.5 meters, and designed to withstand bombs weighing up to a ton, the roof covering the submarine pens was strengthened by an additional 35cm slab of concrete at the beginning of 1942, making the ensemble almost indestructible. Indeed, by the time of the surrender of the St Nazaire pocket in May 1945, the base presented the astonishing spectacle of a gigantic block of intact concrete in the middle of a sea of ruins.

St Nazaire and its environs had been on German time since 1940. The Grand Café at the Place des Quatre Horloges had been transformed into a *Soldatenheim* (a soldiers' home). The Trianon cinema was also requisitioned for the pleasure of the occupation troops, and during leisure time between missions, the submariners could also visit the brothels in and around the city, as well as cabarets in hotels basements at nearby La Baule, where they could even listen to jazz, the "Negro music" officially banned by the Nazi regime. This seaside resort located near St Nazaire became one of the Kriegsmarine's favorite destinations because, nighttime activities aside, the outdoor facilities were reserved exclusively for their use: tennis courts, an equestrian club, a yacht club, a golf course, and the like. Indeed, classified as a "Strategic Coastal Zone" in October 1941, this sector was completely off limits to holidaymakers and locals.

Thanks to their "confined space allowance" and "dive allowance," submariners were significantly better paid than most surface personnel. That said, submariner mortality rates were particularly high: out of a total of 39,000 who served, 27,000 did not return home.

Lieutenant-Commander Erich Topp's *U-552* prepares to berth in submarine pen 12, a wet dock that could accommodate two submarines. (Unknown/ECPAD/Defense)

Some of the *U-552* crew on their arrival at St Nazaire. Mail delivery has just taken place and one of the men is holding a letter. (Unknown/ECPAD/Defense)

This photo taken from the quay shows a submarine at the Southern Entrance. On its turret is the roaring bull of Scapa Flow, the emblem of the 7th U-boat Flotilla.

Each submarine arrival, returning from a mission, was marked with a special ceremony. After crossing beneath the bascule bridge and entering the old basin that was surrounded by houses, the crew lined up at attention on deck, turret adorned with victory pennants, to be greeted by a military band. Nazi propaganda photographers and cameramen, of course, didn't miss a minute of the show. Young women, often Reich nurses, boarded to shower the heroes of the day with garlands of flowers, while officers in dress uniform gave out accolades, awarded medals, and made speeches.

As the submarine fleet too had its heroes, they were worshipped in just the same manner as Reichsmarschall Göring's pilots. Like Günther Prien, who died in March 1941, Heinrich Lehmann-Willenbrock and Erich Topp, two aces of the 7th U-boat Flotilla, were among the most filmed and most photographed submarine commanders documented by Joseph Goebbels's propaganda machine.

From the moment they arrived, the Germans worked tirelessly to fortify the Loire estuary. At its extremities, they installed radar systems to detect any incoming attack—day or night, clear or cloudy, by sea or by sky. Located on the St Gildas promontory, the Würzburg See Riese FuMo 214, with a dish 7.5 meters in diameter, had a range of 60 kilometers. This

Southern Entrance lock, winter 1941. This photo shows three of the four submarines moored together on their return from duty to welcome the 7th U-boat Flotilla commander, Lieutenant-Commander Herbert Sohler. (St Nazaire Municipal Archives)

Two German nurses salute a departing submarine. (St Nazaire Ecomuseum)

A submarine pen today. (Laurent Lemel)

surveillance system was supplemented by land-facing lookouts and by the semaphore operators located on the Chémoulin point, near Pornichet, to the west of St Nazaire.

From Batz-sur-Mer to the Pornic headland, the estuary was surrounded by the coastal batteries of the 280th Naval Artillery Battalion, commanded by Commander Edo Dieckman, whose command post was at Chemoulin. This unit had 30 guns, ranging from 7.5 to 17cm, plus a powerful 24cm battery on tracks, stationed at La Baule.

It was no coincidence that the majority of these pieces were located on the northern shore. Only a few hundred meters from this coastline is the Charpentiers Channel, the only deep-water channel in this vast, muddy region where—even at high tide—the water never exceeds three meters in depth. It was so closely watched and guarded that any vessel attempting to approach the Charpentiers Channel would be spotted immediately, prompting intense fire from the shore-based batteries.

Any assailant arriving by sea would also have to face or evade the various warships patrolling the area: destroyers, Möwe-class torpedo boats and minesweepers, not to mention the harbor defense flotilla of fishing boats, requisitioned and armed by the Kriegsmarine.

If a would-be attacker did, however, manage to reach the port, he would then be faced with obstacles of an even greater magnitude. In addition to underwater nets, curtains of barbed wire stretching across the shoreline, tethered balloons and magnetic mines, the area was littered with bunkers and machine-gun nests.

The 22nd Naval Flak Brigade, commanded by Captain Karl-Conrad Mecke, boasted a total of 43 2cm, 3.7cm, and 4cm guns covering the entire port area, located on the piers

Members of the 2nd Marine War Reporter (Kriegsberichter) Company assemble to receive decorations from Lieutenant Heinrich Schwich. (Unknown/ECPAD/Defense)

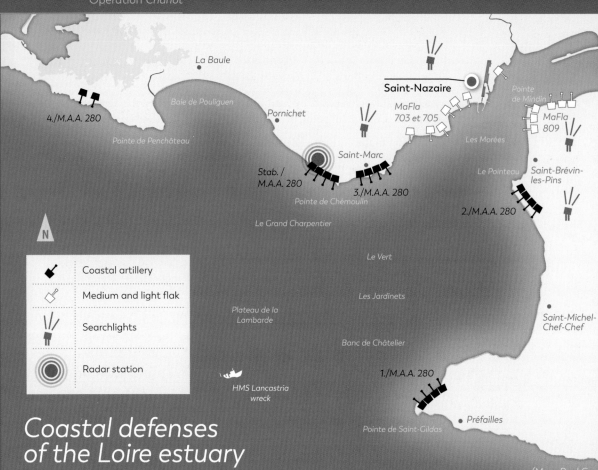

La Baule

Baie de Pouliguen

Pornichet

Pointe de Penchâteau

4./M.A.A. 280

Saint-Nazaire

MaFla
703 et 705

Pointe
de Mindin

MaFla
809

Les Morées

Saint-Marc

Stab. /
M.A.A. 280

3./M.A.A. 280

Pointe de Chémoulin

Le Grand Charpentier

Le Pointeau

Saint-Brévin-
les-Pins

2./M.A.A. 280

N

Le Vert

Coastal artillery

Medium and light flak

Searchlights

Radar station

Les Jardinets

Plateau de la
Lambarde

Banc de Châtelier

Saint-Michel-
Chef-Chef

HMS Lancastria
wreck

1./M.A.A. 280

Coastal defenses
of the Loire estuary

Pointe de Saint-Gildas

Préfailles

(Map: Paul Gros

The Loire estuary: mudflats, shoals,
and sandbars. (Mathieu Poiron)

of the outer harbor, on the Old Mole jetty, on the quays, on both sides of the Joubert lock's outer caisson, on the roof of the cold-storage warehouse and on the roof of the base itself. Many of these pieces were installed on top of concrete shelters, making them difficult to neutralize from sea level.

Thanks to the aerial photographs and information obtained with the help of the local Resistance, Mountbatten's force was at least partially aware of how advanced the German defenses had become. They also knew that the Germans had withdrawn troops from the coast and deployed them inland, north of St Nazaire. However, their intelligence on the subject was far from complete. For example, while the British were able to pinpoint the coastal batteries surrounding the estuary, they knew very little about the smaller-caliber pieces, which were difficult to identify in the aerial photographs.

Similarly, while they followed the construction of bunkers on both sides of the estuary, as on the port, they were sorely lacking in details concerning the armament of these new structures. Did these emplacements house antiaircraft guns or coastal batteries? While this detail may seem secondary at first glance, it takes on a new significance when one considers the plan to send several hundred men to attack such a vast, well-defended fortress.

The Germans had some 6,000 men defending St Nazaire, which itself had some 50,000 inhabitants. In addition to the sailors, there was a full brigade of the 333th Infantry Division stationed inland, but whose command post was located at La Baule. There were also two companies of workers, small units of technicians who were also trained in combat, as well as the crews of the five small tugs stationed in the old basin, plus those of three tankers under repair (two of them in the Joubert lock), all capable of taking up arms in the event of an attack.

Six thousand men against a few hundred British sailors and commandos: the raid on St Nazaire was turning out to be by far the most difficult and risky mission that Combined Operations had ever faced.

German soldiers assigned to defend the port. A 2cm Flak piece is visible in the wooden emplacement among the girders. (St Nazaire Ecomuseum)

The destroyer *Campbeltown* being processed in Plymouth harbor. Note the armor plates added to its deck to protect the commandos it carried. Two 20mm rapid-fire Oerlikon guns were installed on platforms amidships. (The National Archives)

Combining Strike Power and the Element of Surprise

Lord Mountbatten had to kill two birds with one stone: first, sailing as discreetly as possible to reach St Nazaire without alerting the Germans, and second, having the necessary strike force to destroy the port facilities.

Mountbatten and his team soon realized that a commando operation against St Nazaire would only succeed if it combined two major strengths, each as indispensable as the other: surprise and strike power. Without the element of surprise, it would be impossible for the flotilla to reach the Loire estuary, to enter it and to reach the port of St Nazaire without attracting the fire of the innumerable coastal batteries. It was vital that the Germans had their eyes averted while the British were making their long and perilous advance to the port.

There was only one way to accomplish this: a diversion, an aerial bombardment long enough and fierce enough to monopolize the enemy's attention during the assault on the port area.

That was the element of surprise taken care of: next was strike power. The information provided by the local Resistance and the photographs taken by the reconnaissance aircraft had convinced Combined Operations that no conventional means of destruction could reduce the huge steel sliding doors of the Normandie Dock. An alternative had to be found.

At the beginning of February 1942, the naval commander John Hughes-Hallett presented Lord Mountbatten the plan he had drafted, drawn from all the elements collated by Combined Operations. It read roughly as follows: an old destroyer of low draft, loaded with explosives in the front and carrying commandos, would push through the torpedo net protecting the Joubert lock before ramming into and opening up the outer caisson. It would be followed through the breach by a specially equipped torpedo boat, which would take out the inner caisson of the huge dry dock. In the meantime, the commandos would disembark and proceed to destroy the lock gates leading to the old basin. Bomber Command would be tasked with occupying the enemy artillery, searchlights and radar during a bombardment, which would begin before the ships entered the estuary and continue throughout the assault. As for the destroyer used as ram, it would explode after the disembarkation of the men on board, thanks to a system of time bombs. Once the operation was over, the commandos and the crew of the sacrificed destroyer would be collected by a second destroyer.

As seen here, the front of the *Campbeltown* has been significantly modified. Armor plates have been welded to the forecastle to better protect the bridge. A 76.2mm gun replaced the original 100mm gun, which had a slower rate of fire. (The National Archives)

The two main features of the mission decided, other important parameters then had to be taken into account. In addition to the high tide required to cross the estuary without running aground on a sandbar, the raiders would need enough natural light to find their way into the port. It was therefore necessary to study the tides and the moon phases very closely, factoring in the requirement that the naval force had to be undetectable from ground level between dusk and dawn.

Experts at the Liverpool Tidal Institute, who were consulted on the matter, concluded that the most favorable period would be at the end of March, which would see both a high tide and a full moon between midnight and 0200 hours. More specifically, the ideal date would be the night of the 29th/30th. The five nights following that would be acceptable, but any later and the progressive shortening of the nights would render the operation impossible until the autumn.

As the Admiralty was reluctant to sacrifice one of its own destroyers, Mountbatten had to look elsewhere for an appropriate vessel to use as a ram. He decided to petition General Charles de Gaulle in person for the use of the *Ouragan* (Hurricane), a torpedo boat belonging to the Free French. As for the second destroyer, command decided to replace it with a flotilla of some10 Fairmile B Motor Launches. This alternative was not particularly

British sailors on the *Campbeltown*'s forecastle during the ship's conversion. Note on the right, behind the searchlight, one of two 12.7mm Vickers machine guns installed on the forecastle. (The National Archives)

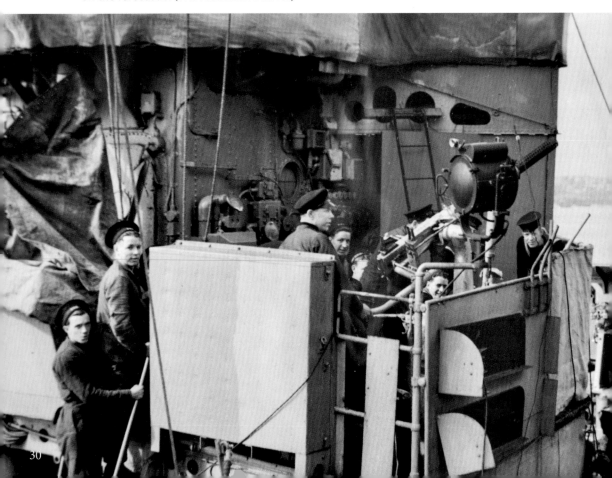

MOST SECRET

Copy No. 3

No. P.76
Combined Operations Headquarters,
War Cabinet Annexe,
1A Richmond Terrace, S.W.1.

27th February 1942

MINUTES OF MEETING HELD AT C.O.H.Q. 1500 hrs 26.2.42. TO
DISCUSS OPERATION "CHARIOT"

Present: PART I

Commodore The Lord Louis Mountbatten (In the Chair)	C.C.O.
Admiral of the Fleet Sir Charles M. Forbes	C. in C. Plymouth
Rear Admiral A.J.Power	A.C.N.S. (H)
Rear Admiral H.E.Horan	R.A.L.B.
Brigadier J.C.Haydon	M.A.C.O.
Brigadier G.E.Wildman-Lushington, P.M.	R.M.A.C.O.
Capt (E) A.L.P. Mark-Wardlaw, R.N.	S.E.O.C.O.
Capt. J.Hughes Hallett R.N.	N.A.C.O.
Capt. D.M.Lees R.N.	D.D.O.D.(C) Admiralty
Capt. C.W.L.Meynell R.N.	C.S.O. to R.A.C.F.
Group Capt A.H.Willetts, R.A.F.	A.A.C.O.
Lt. Col. A.C.Newman	No.2 Commando
Cdr. C.R. McCrumm, R.N.	S.O.O. Plymouth
Comdr. M.Hodges, R.N.	S.O.C.O.
Comdr. G.A.F. Norfolk, R.N.	D.T.M. Admiralty
Comdr. J.R.Westmacott, R.N.	O.D. Admiralty
Comdr J.D.Luce, R.N.	S.O.O.(B) C.O.
Comdr. R.E.D.Ryder, R.N.	Naval Force Comdr.
Major H.M. de B. Romilly	G.2(A) C.O.
Wing Cdr The Marquis of Casa Maury, R.A.F.V.R.	S.I.O.C.O.
Lt. Cdr. L.H.Moorhouse R.N.R.	S.O.I.(N) C.O.
Capt. P.Young	G.2(B) C.O.
Capt. T.M.Gray R.M.	Plan. Sec. C.O.

C.C.O. gave the outline plan for CHARIOT and stated that the
Chiefs of Staff had given their approval but wished to avoid
including vessels manned by the Free French.

2.   C-inC., Plymouth, expressed the opinion that if the longer
route was taken the vessels of the expedition could not hope to
escape detection and attack by aircraft on each of the two days'
approach.   On the other hand, if the shorter route were taken
the vessels would be within the range of enemy fighter aircraft.

3.   It was agreed that the expendable ship must be something that
has the appearance of a destroyer or submarine and should in no
way resemble an assault ship.   A.C.N.S.(H) agreed to explore the
possibilities of finding a suitable ship of this type, or
alternatively a submarine.   The limit of draught to be 12 ft.
It was agreed that a submarine offered the best chance of escaping
detection, but that a destroyer was preferable.

4.   It was agreed that Commander R.E.D.Ryder should be the Naval
Force Commander under the directions of the C-in-C. Plymouth, and
should deal with the C.C.O. and the Admiralty Departments
responsible for manning the vessel and also for any special
training required.

5.   Commander Westmacott (Operations Division) stated that D.N.O.
had already been requested to provide mountings for Oerlikons.
It was agreed that each M.L. should have one Oerlikon fitted in
lieu of the Rolls Gun, and a second one in lieu of the 3 pdr.
R.A.L.B. undertook to investigate the possibility of obtaining the
necessary mountings on vessels already under the command of C.C.O.

The first page of the "Most Secret" minutes from the meeting held on February 26, 1942 at Richmond Terrace, Combined Operations HQ. The number and quality of the participants testify to the importance of this meeting, which was convened to finalize the main points of Operation *Chariot*. (The National Archives)

appealing to the mission planners. While the motorboats offered the advantage of having a shallow draft, and therefore the ability to negotiate the shoals of the Loire estuary, they had two major drawbacks. Built entirely of mahogany and propelled by a gas engine, these boats weighed 90 tons and measured 34.5 meters long and 5.5 meters wide, and could ignite like dry tinder under enemy gunfire. The risk was compounded by the presence of two additional fuel tanks on the deck of each vessel, necessary to help the boats overcome their relative lack of autonomy in terms of mobility.

The other concern for Mountbatten and his deputies was the armament at their disposal. Their unique 47mm Hotchkiss guns and double Lewis machine guns might not be enough to compete with the Luftwaffe and the powerful coastal batteries on the Loire estuary.

On February 19, it was decided that the diversionary bombardment would begin with a heavy shelling of the port area, then move to the city after the landing of the assault and demolition groups. Five days later, Bomber Command HQ proposed that 24 medium bombers attack the port area between 0 hour (entry into the Normandie Dock) and 0 hour–15 minutes; then that 36 medium bombers target the city itself, between 0 hour–15 minutes and 0 hour+2 hours.

Convinced that the *Tirpitz* would soon be ranging in the Atlantic, all guns blazing, the British authorities escalated the raid against St Nazaire to the highest priority. On Thursday, February 26 at 1500, a meeting was held at Richmond Terrace, the number and quality of participants a testament to the importance of the agenda. As well as Mountbatten, attendants included Admiral of the Fleet Sir Charles Forbes, accompanied by several Royal Navy officers, including Rear Admiral John Power, Deputy Chief of the Naval Staff; Major-General Joseph (Charles) Haydon, commander of the Special Service Brigade; and Group Captain Arthur Willetts, representing the RAF. Including Mountbatten's senior officers, there was a total of around twenty general staff officers.

Using his model of the port, Mountbatten began proceedings by outlining the operation, now codenamed *Chariot*. Admiral Forbes expressed particular concern about the choice of the route to the port. It was essential, he explained, to map a sea route that was not too long, but that was sufficient to avoid naval patrols and aerial attacks.

Another important decision to be made was what vessel to use as a ram. Not wanting to use the Gaullist *Ouragan*, the Admiralty had still not provided a destroyer. They did consider employing a large submarine, "which would offer the best chance of escaping detection." However, a destroyer remained the preferable option. Now there was just the small matter of finding one.

Fairmile B Motor Launches had the advantage of having a shallow draft, but their mahogany frames made them particularly vulnerable to artillery fire. (Imperial War Museum)

MOST SECRET

P.76/354

24th February, 1942.

To: **The Chiefs of Staff Committee**

OPERATION CHARIOT

Approval is requested to carry out a Combined Operation against ST. NAZAIRE, an outline of which is attached. It will be noticed that an expendable destroyer is required. I would prefer an old British destroyer to avoid bringing in the Free French but if it is decided that a French destroyer is to be used, it is suggested that I should be authorised to approach General de Gaulle in person.

(sgd) LOUIS MOUNTBATTEN

C.C.O.
Adviser on Combined Operations.

In this "Most Secret" note dated February 24, 1942, Lord Mountbatten mentions the possibility of asking General de Gaulle for a Free French destroyer to serve as a ram against the outer caisson of the Joubert lock. (The National Archives)

To increase the firepower of the speedboats carrying the commandos, the naval officers decided to replace the usual 3-pounders with 20mm rapid-fire Oerlikon cannons.

For the duration of their training, which would last right up until they left Falmouth for France, the commandos would be using the HMS *Princess Josephine-Charlotte*, a troop transport, as a base. To prepare for the voyage, the commandos would have to make several long rehearsal trips aboard the speedboats, of which there were currently twelve.

At the end of this meeting, Major-General Haydon introduced the two men selected to lead Operation *Chariot*: for the land-based part of the operation, Lieutenant-Colonel Charles Newman, and for the naval component, Commander Robert Ryder.

Charles Newman appeared older than his 38 years, what with his round face adorned with a small mustache, his squat silhouette and receding hairline. But appearances can be deceptive: this amiable-looking family man was an elite officer, whose natural authority, charisma and good humor made him a true leader of men. Newman was the founder and leader of No. 2 Commando, two troops of which had participated in the successful Operation *Archery* on Vaagso, Norway, in December 1941. Back in their billets at Ayr in southern Scotland, No. 2 Commando, and Newman in particular, were now waiting for one thing: a new mission, at least as bold and "sporting" as the one they had conducted in Norway.

With his square face, rigid regard, and dry voice, Commander Robert Edward Dudley Ryder seemed at first glance to be the exact opposite of Newman. At 34, "Red" (so nicknamed because of his initials, R.E.D.) was already an old seadog. He had joined the Royal Navy at 18, and rose quickly through the ranks, thanks to his keen sense of duty, his great aptitude for command and his undeniable skill as a sailor. He had already, among other assignments,

The stern of *Campbeltown* during its conversion in Plymouth harbor. In the foreground are two Carley life rafts, securely moored. (The National Archives)

served in the submarines, led a two-year scientific expedition to the Antarctic, served on a battleship in the Mediterranean and commanded an armed merchant ship tasked with attracting and sinking German submarines in the Irish Sea. But the star of this promising officer had started to fade in the summer of 1941, after his ship, the *Prince Philippe*, a troop transport, was approached and sunk in thick fog by another British ship, just off the coast of Scotland, in the Firth of Clyde. Deprived of a sea command, Ryder found himself at Wilton House, near Salisbury, assigned to the staff of Sir Harold Alexander, General Officer Commanding-in-Chief Southern Command, advising in naval matters concerning defense against invasion.

By early 1942, both Ryder and Newman were desperate to get back into action. Despite their different backgrounds, these two men, both animated by the same patriotic ideals and endowed with the same relentless energy, bonded instantly. As soon as they met, they got to work. They had only a month to pull everything together, from the composition of the assault group to the return trip, the training of the commandos, the preparation of equipment and the planning, to the nth degree, and the different phases of the attack on St Nazaire's port facilities.

One of the first issues to be settled was the destruction of the Joubert lock, the main objective of the mission. A suitable destroyer had still not been found, and using a submarine did not appeal to Newman and Ryder at all. After studying the available submarines, they quickly came to the conclusion that none was up to the job. It would be far too difficult for the commandos, loaded as they would be with explosives and weapons, to quickly disembark the vessel after breaking through the outer caisson of the Normandie Dock. Moreover, it seemed obvious to the two commanders that the three days spent in the cramped cabin and the confined atmosphere of a submarine would have a severely detrimental effect on the physical and psychological health of the commandos, who had to be at the top of their game from the instant they stepped onto *terra firma*.

Reluctant to see the operation canceled, however, Newman and Ryder worked on a third option, which they presented on Tuesday, March 3, at a planning meeting at Richmond Terrace. It consisted of using light speedboats to carry enough commandos to destroy the gates with their own explosives. The two commanders explained that speedboats would have the twofold advantage of being able to navigate the shoals, and being more difficult to spot than a large ship. John Hughes-Hallet was not convinced, and noted the vulnerability of the wooden boats to the German coastal batteries in the Loire estuary.

Mountbatten, too, opposed the idea of using speedboats, and preferred the destroyer option. A few days later, the long-awaited news arrived: a ram boat had finally been found. It was the *Campbeltown*, built in the United States in 1918. In its earlier life, the 95-meter-long ship had served in the US Navy under the name of *Buchanan*, from 1919 to mid-June 1940. It was then part of a group of 50 "obsolete" destroyers donated by the US government to Great Britain in exchange for access to British ports in the West Indies.

To make the *Campbeltown* look more like a German Möwe-class torpedo boat, two of its four funnels were removed and the remaining two beveled. In the foreground, under tarpaulins, are probably the 20mm Oerlikon rapid-fire guns, the same model as those installed on "bandstands" amidships. (The National Archives)

Immediately, Newman and Ryder traveled to Southampton to view the ship that would be the centerpiece of Operation *Chariot*. It was with some dismay that they discovered four prominent funnels on its forecastle; its easily recognizable shape would quickly identify it to enemy aircraft. It would be suicidal to approach St Nazaire with the *Campbeltown* in this, its original, configuration. To deceive the German lookouts for the longest possible time, they had to make it appear as one of the commonest ships serving in the Kriegsmarine, which were Möwe-class torpedo boats, of comparable length and tonnage to the *Campbeltown*, operating in the Atlantic out of French ports. RAF reconnaissance had spotted four of them at anchor in the St Nazaire basin.

On March 10, the *Campbeltown* was transferred to Plymouth harbor, where reconstruction work began the same day. To give the old destroyer the shape of a German torpedo boat, engineers began by removing two of its four funnels; those remaining were beveled and inclined backward. In addition to changing its appearance, it was necessary to lighten the vessel so that it could negotiate the shoals of the estuary without bottoming out. Water and fuel reserves were minimized and the ship freed of unnecessary equipment and armaments, such as torpedo tubes and depth charges. The aim was to reduce the draft from 4.3 meters to 3.2 meters, a decrease deemed necessary by Royal Navy navigational experts to clear the shoals. The experts also predicted that, once stripped down, the *Campbeltown* would only have a 60-centimeter clearance at high tide. This was really cutting it fine, so the crew would have to be extremely careful during the final phase of the long journey from England.

The midship area of the *Campbeltown* during its conversion in Plymouth harbor. (The National Archives)

MOST SECRET   1 / 6

2.3 42.

6.   OPERATION "CHARIOT".

(Previous Reference: C.O.S.(42) 68th Meeting,
                                    Minute 1.)

     LORD LOUIS MOUNTBATTEN said that the success
of Operation "Chariot" depended very largely on the
success of the diversion created by air bombing.
He was anxious for a ruling as to whether or not
the Operation should be postponed if the force had
sailed and it was then found that air action was
impossible on account of adverse weather. There was
nothing to indicate that the force was part of a
combined operation and he considered that the
secrecy of a "repeat" operation was unlikely to be
compromised by the early return of the force after it
had sailed.

     THE COMMITTEE:-

     Agreed that Operation "Chariot" should not be
     undertaken unless the diversionary air bombing
     could be carried out.

94th Meeting on 24/3/42.

In this "Most Secret" letter, dated March 3, 1942, Lord Mountbatten insists on the importance of a diversionary aerial bombardment for the success of Operation *Chariot*. (The National Archives)

The onboard firepower also underwent significant change. At the bow, a 75mm gun replaced the original 100mm gun. Eight 20mm Oerlikon cannons, mounted on platforms known as "bandstands," were distributed along the deck, between the funnels and the stern. Amidships, steel barriers were installed to allow the soldiers to brace themselves for the collision on ramming.

Similarly, the bridge was surrounded by armor plating of a carefully calculated thickness, strong but not so heavy as to weigh down the structure. On each side of the forecastle were Vickers 12.7mm machine guns with a firing rate of 700 rounds per minute.

Newman and Ryder were assisted in their task by Lieutenant Nigel Tibbits (28), chosen to turn *Campbeltown* into a floating bomb of phenomenal power. Tibbits, son of an admiral, was a recognized specialist in the field of explosives. He was top of his class at HMS *Vernon*, a Royal Navy shore establishment in Portsmouth, where torpedoes, mines and other means of destruction had been studied since 1876.

At Tibbits's insistence, the original plan of having the commandos place explosives immediately after the collision was abandoned. *Chariot*'s new naval expert had no trouble convincing his colleagues that it was too risky to consider carrying explosives from the *Campbeltown* to the outer caisson of the Normandie Dock under enemy fire, before taking up precious time to set the timers.

One of the first problems Tibbits faced was determining the ideal positioning of the explosive charge on board the destroyer. It had to be placed far enough back not to be damaged during the collision, but close enough to the bow to impact its target efficiently.

Finally, he decided to place the charge just behind the steel beam supporting the forward gun turret. Consisting of 24 depth charges, each one weighing 400 pounds, or 180 kilograms, and thus amounting to just under five tons of explosives, the charge was enclosed in a steel tank located above the fuel tanks and cemented into the hull.

As for the firepower, Tibbits decided on a brand-new model of a long-range rocket, the "Pencil." These would be primed at around 2300, before the boat entered the estuary, and set on a timer to go off eight hours later. Finally, the decision was made to scuttle the ship as soon as it broke through the caisson, to prevent any German attempts to defuse it and making it impossible for them to move it.

Tibbits was assisted by Captain William Pritchard of the Royal Engineers (RE). This 28-year-old Welshman had made a name for himself in June 1940 by blowing up a bridge under enemy fire during the Dunkirk evacuations, an accomplishment that earned him the Military Cross. Moreover, Pritchard was already familiar with St Nazaire, having landed there with the British Expeditionary Force in September 1939. Most importantly, he had an interesting and original theory on the issue that had been obsessing Newman and Ryder since they took command of *Chariot*. It occurred to him one day when he was on leave and witnessed a massive Luftwaffe attack on Cardiff harbor. Noting that the bombing had caused spectacular but ultimately insignificant damage to the harbor's infrastructure, the pragmatic Pritchard came to the conclusion that the best way to render a port inoperative was not to

Two more Oerlikon firing positions located aft. (The National Archives)

The pumping station today. (J-C Stasi)

bombard it from the air, but rather to methodically destroy any major installations from the ground by means of explosive charges.

Pritchard refined this theory with the help of Robert Montgomery, an RE captain with whom he had been friendly while serving as an instructor at Aldershot. Together, the two officers worked extensively on British and foreign port plans, without knowing which was which, assessing the number of men and calculating the quantities of explosives needed to destroy each.

As soon as he arrived at Richmond Terrace, Pritchard was given responsibility for the destruction of the port facilities at St Nazaire. At his side was Montgomery, and the pair got to work immediately, only too aware of the immensity of the task facing them. Before reembarking, the *Chariot* munitions specialists had to silence guns, demolish buildings, cranes and ships, and disable the pump-station infrastructure located ten meters underground. The permutations were boundless: there were so many different objectives requiring different types and amounts of explosives, and different detonation systems. As if that were not enough, they also had to consider what would happen if the *Campbeltown* could not fulfill its mission for one reason or another, forcing the planners to figure out how much extra explosives each man would have to carry to demolish the outer caisson of the Joubert lock in addition to the inner door.

In Profile:
HMS *Campbeltown*

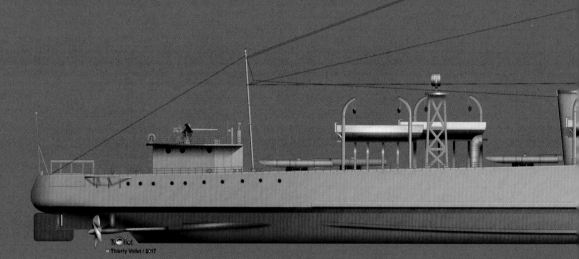

HMS *Campbeltown* in its original configuration, as it appeared when it was donated to the Royal Navy by the US Navy in the summer of 1940 (then named the USS *Buchanan*).

HMS *Campbeltown* after its conversion into a Mowe-type torpedo boat. Its shape, style, defenses, and armament were all significantly altered.

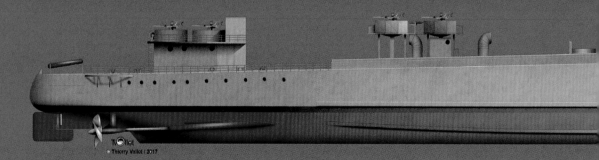

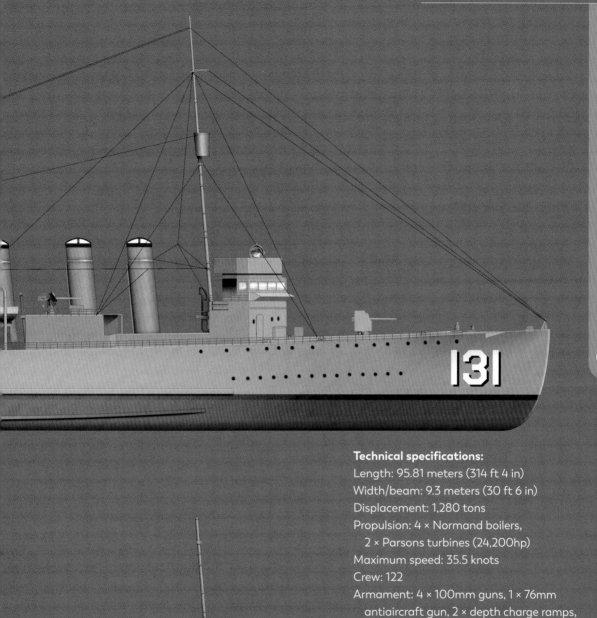

Technical specifications:
Length: 95.81 meters (314 ft 4 in)
Width/beam: 9.3 meters (30 ft 6 in)
Displacement: 1,280 tons
Propulsion: 4 × Normand boilers,
   2 × Parsons turbines (24,200hp)
Maximum speed: 35.5 knots
Crew: 122
Armament: 4 × 100mm guns, 1 × 76mm
   antiaircraft gun, 2 × depth charge ramps,
   12 × 533mm-diameter torpedo tubes
          (Thierry Vallet)

Commandos in a landing craft going ashore during training in Scotland, February 28, 1942. (Lts W. T. Lockeyear, E. G. Malindine / IWM H17472)

In Profile:
Lieutenant-Colonel Charles Newman VC

Lieutenant-Colonel Charles Newman VC, OBE, TD, DL was born in Chingwell, Essex, UK on August 19, 1904. On the outbreak of war, he was serving with the Essex Regiment (Territorial Army); at the time of Operation *Chariot*, he was the commanding officer of No. 2 Commando, which is where he earned the Victoria Cross. His citation in the *London Gazette* reads in part:

> Coolly and calmly he stood on the bridge of the leading craft, as the small force steamed up the estuary of the River Loire, although the ships had been caught in the enemy searchlights and a murderous cross-fire opened from both banks, causing heavy casualties.

> Although Lieutenant-Colonel Newman need not have landed himself, he was one of the first ashore and, during the next five hours of bitter fighting, he personally entered several houses and shot up the occupants and supervised the operations in the town, utterly regardless of his own safety, and he never wavered in his resolution to carry through the operation upon which so much depended.

> An enemy gun position on the roof of a U-boat pen had been causing heavy casualties to the landing craft and Lieutenant-Colonel Newman directed the fire of a mortar against this position to such effect that the gun was silenced. Still fully exposed, he then brought machine gun fire to bear on an armed trawler in the harbour, compelling it to withdraw and thus preventing many casualties in the main demolition area.

> Under the brilliant leadership of this officer the troops fought magnificently and held vastly superior enemy forces at bay, until the demolition parties had successfully completed their work of destruction.

Following his service with the Commandos, Newman served as CO 21st Special Air Service Regiment (Artists) and as Major in the Engineer and Railway Staff Corps, until 1959. Also the recipient of the French Legion d'Honneur and the Croix de Guerre, he died aged 72 at Sandwich, Kent in 1972.

Newman and Ryder on All Fronts

In late February 1942, the two commanders of Operation *Chariot* were engaged in a frantic race against the clock. They had just one month to organize every last detail of the raid, from the composition of the assault and demolition groups to the logistics of the return journey.

The task given by Lord Mountbatten to Charles Newman and Robert Ryder was enormous. But knowing that *Chariot* was undoubtedly the most daring operation they would ever command, the two officers threw everything they had into the mission. They were bolstered by the success of Operation *Biting*, launched by Combined Operations the day after the meeting at Richmond Terrace, when, on the night of February 27/28, British paratroopers attacked the Bruneval radar station, situated on top of a cliff, a few kilometers from Le Havre. Sustaining only minor losses, Major J. D. Frost's men managed to return to England by sea, having taken one German radar technician prisoner and uplifted some vital components of the radar system.

To assist in the matters of organization and planning, Newman summoned the Adjutant-General of No. 2 Commando, Stanley Day. At the same time, he entrusted the training of the protection and assault groups to his second-in-command, Major William

In Scotland, commandos practice landing under a smokescreen. (The National Archives)

Copland. At 42, this veteran of the Great War, affectionately nicknamed "Major Bill" by his soldiers, was known for his courage and level head.

Each protection squad was composed of an officer and four men armed with sub-machine guns. The assault groups were generally composed of two officers and 12 men apiece, equipped with sub-machine guns and rifles.

As for the 90 men selected to form the demolition teams, they were entrusted to William Pritchard and Robert Montgomery, Nigel Tibbits being occupied with the conversion of the *Campbeltown* at the Devonport shipyard in Plymouth. In addition to Lieutenant-Colonel Newman's No. 2 Commando, they included elements from units of the Special Service Brigade, namely Commandos 1, 3, 4, 5, 9, and 12.

For the most part, the men participating in Operation *Chariot* were not professional soldiers and came from very different professional backgrounds: a history student, an attorney, a stockbroker, a teacher, a political economics graduate, a bank clerk, and even a renowned archaeologist. But whether they were veterans of Dunkirk or Norway, or had learned the exploits of the commandos in the newspapers or on newsreels, all shared a deep desire to deal a severe blow to the Germans.

Under the watchful eye of Major Copland, the men of No. 2 Commando began training at a feverish pace in Scotland: climbing the snowy slopes of the Highlands with full equipment; trekking up to a hundred kilometers in a 24-hour period across the moors, battered by wind and rain; rehearsing landings in the icy waters of the lochs; crossing rivers

Lieutenant-Colonel Charles Newman, commander of No. 2 Commando, was chosen to direct the land-based part of Operation *Chariot*. (The National Archives)

As he was so busy organizing the raid, Newman gave his deputy, Major Bill Copland, the task of training the commandos who would be landing at St Nazaire. (Peter Copland and Commando Veterans Association)

on rope bridges; practicing close-quarter combat in deserted villages; and training to shoot with any and every weapon available to them.

The commandos refined their preparations by simulating the attack on an oil refinery after disembarking from assault boats. To help them gain their sea legs and to teach them how to shoot in maritime conditions, they were engaged as a protective force on real convoy escort vessels. The less experienced commandos were even taken on field trips to a slaughterhouse and a field hospital to familiarize them with the smell and sight of blood.

Demolition crews also began training on the east coast of Scotland. In the dry dock at Rosyth port, they learned how to operate the caisson doors—and how to neutralize them. In particular, they were taught how to place the plastic charges on the doors' most vulnerable points, mold the malleable explosives around the sections to be destroyed, lay the fuses, and finally detonate the charges using a "safety line" or by hand.

When this first phase of training was complete, the demolition teams were then sent to Cardiff and Southampton to continue training in conditions similar to those they would experience in the field, though they were unaware of what or where the target was. This step-up in training was accompanied by a tightening of security measures. This time, uniforms were stripped of any identifying features; dockers, police, foreign military personnel, and civilians were kept out of the way.

The port of Southampton had the advantage of featuring a dock much like that at St Nazaire: the George V dock, which was large enough to accommodate the *Queen Mary*, a 310-meter-long liner. At this dock, the commandos responsible for the destruction of the Joubert lock caissons tirelessly rehearsed their mission, first of all by day, then blindfolded,

Troops practice close-quarters combat techniques. (The National Archives)

and finally by night. They repeated their actions over and over until they were etched into their brains and their muscle memory. It may sound extreme, but these men had to be capable of carrying out any demolition, in the dark, in under 10 minutes.

Those commandos tasked with taking on the pumping station faced similar trials. Learning to navigate the maze of stairs and corridors, they became familiar with the various machines, transformers, motors, and pumps, repeating the same procedures a hundred times until they perfected placing the explosives at precise points, in the correct manner, and in the fastest possible time.

For his part, Robert Ryder spent countless hours organizing the naval actions of the operation. His task was complicated on several occasions when he was forced him to modify his plans. For example, the number of motorboats being deployed alongside the *Campbeltown* was increased from eight to 16: four more to carry additional commandos demanded by Newman after the discovery of four new large coastal batteries at the port, and a further four armed with 457mm torpedoes to protect the convoy in the event of an attack by a Kriegsmarine patrol.

Ryder also obtained the Admiralty's permission to arm the 16 Fairmile B Motor Launches with 20mm Oerlikon guns in addition to their old Lewis machine guns. To reduce the risk of fire on these wooden craft, Ryder planned to fill the two 2,000-liter auxiliary fuel tanks with seawater once they were empty of fuel. Each motorboat crew was composed of two or three officers, plus a dozen men from the Royal Naval Volunteer Reserve. Among the sailors were volunteers from Canada, New Zealand, and Australia. For Operation *Chariot*, the basic crew of each boat was reinforced with specialists in armaments and navigation, as well as about 15 commandos forming the landing party.

The flotilla included two other light vessels, each with a specific role. The Fairmile MGB (Motor Gun Boat) *314* was chosen to serve as a command ship for Ryder and Newman during the final phase of the crossing. Not only was it faster than the B-type motorboats, it was also better armed, equipped with a Vickers "pom-pom" gun capable of firing 120 rounds per minute, two 13mm double-barreled machine guns in the center and a semi-automatic 47mm Rolls Royce machine gun at the rear. Furthermore, it had radar and an echo sounder, allowing it to lead the rest of the flotilla through the dangerous shoals of the estuary. Although it had many additional fuel tanks, it still had to be towed for the first part of the trip.

Its commander, Lieutenant Dunstan Curtis, a civil litigation attorney, was a regular in high-risk missions. The crew, increased to 24 for the raid, also included Lieutenant-Commander William Green, a specialist in navigation, who had the onerous dual task of guiding the flotilla throughout the crossing, and steering the *Campbeltown* as far as the Normandie Dock. Signal Quartermaster Seymour Pike also played a key role in the approach phase; using the naval code system taken from the Germans in Norway, he would replicate enemy reconnaissance signals in order to delay retaliatory fire from the coastal batteries and Kriegsmarine vessels patrolling the St Nazaire area.

Troops practice close-quarters combat techniques. (The National Archives)

Ryder also saw action in the ill-fated Dieppe Raid. Here the stricken HMS *Berkeley*, crippled by German bombing, is torpedoed by the Royal Navy. (Lt L. Pelman RN / IWM A11244)

In Profile:
Commander Robert Ryder VC

Educated at Cheltenham College in Gloucestershire, England, Captain Robert Edward Dudley Ryder VC was born in India, in 1908, his father Colonel Charles Ryder being Surveyor General of the subcontinent. Both Ryder's brothers died serving during World War II. Prior to 1939, Ryder served as a midshipman on the battleship HMS *Ramillies* (1927–29), as a lieutenant on the submarine HMS *Olympus* (1930–33) and captained the schooner *Penoia* on the Graham Land Expedition to Antarctica (1934–37).

On the outbreak of the World War II, in 1939, he found himself a lieutenant-commander on HMS *Warspite* before being promoted, in 1940, to commander of the Q-ship HMS *Edgehill*. Torpedoed in the middle of the Atlantic, Ryder was adrift for four days before being rescued. In early 1941, he assumed command of the troop transport *Prince Philippe* which was sunk after a collision in the Firth of Clyde, on the west coast of Scotland. Rescued from disgrace, he was appointed naval commander on Operation *Chariot* where he was to earn the Victoria Cross, His citation reads in part:

The KING has been graciously pleased to approve the award of the Victoria Cross for daring and valour in the attack on the German Naval Base at St. Nazaire, to:

Commander Robert Edward Dudley Ryder, Royal Navy.

For great gallantry in the attack on St Nazaire. He commanded a force of small unprotected ships in an attack on a heavily defended port and led H.M.S. *Campbeltown* in under intense fire from short range weapons at point blank range. Though the main object of the expedition had been accomplished in the beaching of *Campbeltown*, he remained on the spot conducting operations, [as well as] evacuating men from *Campbeltown* and dealing with strong points and close range weapons while exposed to heavy fire for one hour and sixteen minutes, and did not withdraw till it was certain that his ship could be of no use in rescuing any of the Commando Troops who were still ashore. That his Motor Gun Boat, now full of dead and wounded, should have survived and should have been able to withdraw through an intense barrage of close range fire was almost a miracle.

Ryder also served during the ill-fated Dieppe Raid of August 19, 1942, eventually achieving the rank of captain in 1948. Participating in another Antarctic expedition, he was also naval attaché to Oslo, Norway for a spell, before being elected the Conservative MP for Merton and Morden in 1950. Also the recipient of the French Legion d'Honneur and the Croix de Guerre, he died on June 29, 1986 during a sailing trip to France.

Troops practice close-quarters combat techniques.
(The National Archives)

Completing the flotilla, MTB (Motor Torpedo Boat) *74*, also made of wood, measuring 20 meters in length and weighing 35 tons, was a unique specimen, much like the man who commanded it. Sub-Lieutenant Robert Wynn, better known as "Micky" or "Popeye," was an eccentric Welshman who began his career in the cavalry before transferring to the navy where he distinguished himself by considerably remodeling his ship on his own initiative.

A few weeks earlier, Wynn had had an idea: he could attack the German cruiser *Scharnhorst* in the port of Brest, using powerful torpedoes designed to explode only after passing over the antisubmarine net protecting the heavy battlecruiser. Once the Admiralty gave his plan the go-ahead, Wynn moved the torpedo tubes from the center of MTB *74* to the forecastle.

Unfortunately, the *Scharnhorst* set sail from Brest on the night of February 11 alongside the *Gneisenau* and *Prinz Eugen*, so Wynn was unable to put his plan into action. Luckily for him, his remodeled MTB *74*, which was as destructive as it was fast—it had a top speed of 49 knots, though its engines were somewhat unreliable—caught the attention of the Operation *Chariot* commanders. Without the *Scharnhorst* to tear to pieces, the vessel was free to accompany the flotilla and dispatch two 700kg torpedoes at the outer caisson of the Normandie Dock should the *Campbeltown* fail in its mission.

In mid-March, the assault troops and demolition groups met in Falmouth, southwest England, where the motorboats were already stationed and where HMS *Princess Josephine Charlotte*—a troop transport—had just arrived to serve as a base for the commandos and HQ for Newman and Ryder. The Royal Navy sailors were impressed by the commandos. After the war, Ralph Batteson, a gunner on ML*14*, recalled that they were "tough and resolute and showed lightning-swift reactions when required ... True, they were dressed in a motley assortment of clothing that could hardly be called standard issue, but I knew they had been specially trained and selected for this mission, and were to be relied upon." Batteson remembered that they were a very happy group of men who lived life to the fullest and loved to play practical jokes on each other.

Commandos in training cross a Scottish river during the winter of 1942. (Peter Copland and Commando Veterans Association)

While continuing to prepare for their respective missions, the sailors and commandos got to know each other through joint exercises. On Monday, March 16, at 0900, the motorboats left Falmouth for the Scilly Isles, off the tip of Cornwall, carrying the commandos. On the program was navigation training, both day and night. The weather was abysmal and the mahogany boats were severely shaken about in the poor conditions.

Two days later, the 39 officers of the commando contingent were summoned by Lieutenant-Colonel Newman to a briefing on the *Princess Josephine Charlotte*. With his pipe in his mouth and flanked by his faithful assistants Bill Copland and Stanley Day, Newman stood waiting for them in front of the model of the port facilities and a blackboard, on which was drawn what looked like an estuary but without any context. He began by telling them the codename of the operation, and revealed that their destination was a French port, the name of which would be communicated to them only upon their departure.

He explained that there were twenty-four objectives in total, but that the main objective, more important than any other, was the outer caisson of the large dry dock. The 39 officers would all receive a 40-page order of operations and be briefed individually about their specific mission. He told them that the combat troops had two goals. The first was to attack and destroy enemy artillery positions, then maintain a perimeter delimited by several bridges until all demolitions had been completed and members of those teams had had time to retreat within that perimeter. The second task was to provide close protection to the demolition teams so that they were able to lay and detonate their charges.

Newman explained that the force leaving Falmouth would consist of: two escort destroyers, the *Tynedale* and *Atherstone*; the Campbeltown; MGB *314*, which would serve as the command post; MTB *314* with its delayed-action torpedoes; and 16 Fairmile B Motor Launches, 12 of which would carry commandos and the other four torpedoes. The flotilla would be completed by a submarine, the *Sturgeon*, which would make its way to the estuary separately. Its mission would be to surface when the flotilla arrived to guide it toward the estuary by means of a light affixed to the top of its periscope.

The scheduled time for the landing was 0130. A diversionary air raid on the port was planned for 2200, which would then move to the town itself between midnight and 0130.

The lieutenant-colonel then stated that the commandos would be divided into three groups, each with a specific area of intervention. Groups 1 and 2 would travel on the motorboats and Group 3 aboard the *Campbeltown*. The motorboats would enter the Loire estuary in two columns, either side of *Campbeltown*, Group 1 on the port side and Group 2 on the starboard.

The six Group 1 boats, led by Captain Bertie Hodgson, would land at Old Mole jetty, which had a slipway. In addition to several artillery batteries, his men would have to destroy the gates of the southern entrance to the lock and the pumping station located near the same entrance.

The six motorboats of Group 2, under Captain Michael Burn, including the one carrying Colonel Newman and his staff, would moor at the Old Entrance to the St Nazaire Basin. Once landed, the commandos would then have to disable the lock and the swing

Commandos navigate an obstacle course during training. (The National Archives)

bridge of the Old Entrance, as well as the bascule bridge separating the St Nazaire basin from the Penhoët basin. Burn's men were also tasked with silencing a number of artillery pieces and neutralizing the weaponry on any vessels in the basin.

Group 3, commanded by Major Bill Copland, would also have a lot to do after disembarking the *Campbeltown*. If the old destroyer failed in breaking through the outer caisson of the Normandie Dock, they would to finish the job. In addition, Group 3 would have to deal with the inner caisson, the pumping station and the buildings housing the caisson operating facilities, not to mention the destruction of a number of guns, including those placed on the roof of the pumping station.

Captain Pritchard would lead the demolition team assigned to Groups 1 and 2 and Captain Montgomery would lead the demolition team assigned to Group 3. As soon as their missions were completed, each demolition team would return to Newman's command post, located next to the Old Entrance. Then, once the assault sections joined them, all the troops would converge at the Old Mole jetty for reembarkation. The final boat had to leave the jetty at 0 hour+1 hour 50 minutes. Since they would be working at night, the commandos needed to be able to recognize each other easily, so they used Spanish white to highlight the straps of their equipment. In addition, each man would be equipped with a flashlight emitting blue light, and would respond to being summoned with his commanding officer's name. Finally, Newman had concocted a password that he related to his officers with no small amount of pleasure. He informed them that he had selected the password "War Weapons Week," to which should be replied "Weymouth." He observed "I defy any German to say that correctly."

Before concluding the meeting, Newman added that the commandos would wear the new style of rubber-soled shoes, which were far less noisy than the traditional model. The men therefore knew that if they heard someone's shoes sounding on the ground they could be confident that it was a German, and could move to sound the alarm.

On Saturday, March 21, at the end of the day, sailors and commandos met for their last joint maneuver before the operation. Dubbed *Vivid*, this final rehearsal took place at Devonport, with facilities that were not too dissimilar to those at St Nazaire. Taking on the role of the Germans was the Home Guard, the volunteer defense unit created in May 1940 to protect Britain from German invasion.

The motorboats carrying the assault troops cut silently through the waves in the darkness, any naked flames and lights extinguished. As they began the approach to the docks, things started to take a turn for the worse. The helmsmen were so dazzled by the powerful lights on the flotilla that they had great difficulty staying on course and landing in the right place. Indifferent to this problem, the commandos leapt from the barely moored boats and scattered through the dock area, taking "prisoners" and tying them to cranes and lampposts, as if it were the real operation.

Despite the effective action of Newman's men, this final rehearsal did not prove overly convincing. Observing the maneuvers, Major-General Haydon and his deputy, Major Robert Henriques, realized that *Vivid* was far from a roaring success, though it did at least give the sailors and commandos some glimpse of what awaited them several hundred kilometers

MOST SECRET   5SA 3.16.

TO:-

CONFIDENTIAL.

Training Programme for A/S Sweep

12th Thurs.	M.L's from Portsmouth Command carry out sleeve firing off Weymouth and then proceed to Falmouth. Remainder of M.L's arrive Falmouth P.M.
13th Fri.	P.M. M.L's exercise Station keeping and manouvering under orders of S.O. M.L's M.T.B.74 arrives Plymouth and is towed to Falmouth by H.M.S. PRINCESS JOSEPHIN CHARLOTTE arrives Falmouth with troop.
14th Sat.	M.L's sail at dusk and exercise manouvering after dark returning about 2300 and practice going alongside in the dock area. Under orders of Commander Ryder.
15th	M.L's operating in harbour with exercise landing 9: troops in the dock area - under orders of S.O.M.L'. (2100 to 2300).
16th	0900 - Sail for extended cruise with troops on board M.L's. Exercising day and night formations.
17th	2200 Return to Falmouth. M.G.B.314 arrives Plymouth and is towed to Falmouth the next day.
18th	CAMPBELTOWN with reduced complement sails for Falmouth with M.G.B.314 in tow. STURGEON arrives.
19th	C.O. CAMPBELTOWN to practice handling his ship and going alongside after dark.
20th	Spare day.
21st	Approx.1500 all available forces sail from Falmout so as to arrive off Plymouth Breakwater ½ hour after sunset. Full scale rehearsal of attack on Devonport Dockyard. The force is to withdraw and return to Falmouth by 0400/22. STURGEON being used as navigational beacon.
22nd.	
23rd.	Local night training, going alongside after dark and landing troops.
24th	Sleeve target fiting/or storing.
25th	Sleeve target fiting (spare day)/or storing.
26th	Spare day.

The training schedule for the *Chariot* forces at Falmouth, from March 12 to 26, 1942, the 26th being the day they were due to leave for St Nazaire. (The National Archives)

away, albeit in a far more hostile environment. There was another problem: the diversionary air raid, on which Mountbatten, Newman and Ryder placed great emphasis, was ultimately going to be smaller than anticipated due the reluctance of Bomber Command, who were anxious to retain as many aircraft available as possible for its own missions.

After initially trying to reduce the number of aircraft by half, Bomber Command finally compromised, at the insistence of Lord Mountbatten, agreeing to engage 62 aircraft instead of 70, but the pilots, who knew only that they would be acting in support of "a night operation, carried out by naval and land forces," were not allowed to attack any targets other than those designated or to descend below 6,500 feet. In addition, it was made clear to them that they should not drop their bombs if it was not possible to identify the target.

Seen here is the USS *Buchanan* (DD-131), shortly before transfer to the Royal Navy, on September 9, 1940, when the vessel was renamed HMS *Campbeltown*. In the foreground Royal Navy and US Navy sailors are inspecting depth charges. (Library of Congress ID fsa.8e00843)

In Profile:

Lieutenant-Commander Stephen Beattie VC

Son of a clergyman, Captain Stephen ("Sam") Halden Beattie VC was born in Montgomeryshire, Wales, in 1908. Schooled at Abberley Hall in Worcester, he joined the Royal Navy as a cadet in 1925. Aged 33, he was given command of the HMS *Campbeltown*, the ram ship in Operation *Chariot*, where he was to earn the Victoria Cross, his citation reading in part:

> For great gallantry and determination in the attack on St. Nazaire in command of HMS Campbeltown. Under intense fire directed at the bridge from point blank range of about 100 yards, and in the face of the blinding glare of many searchlights, he steamed her into the lock-gates and

beached and scuttled her in the correct position.

> This Victoria Cross is awarded to Lieutenant-Commander S. H. Beattie in recognition not only of his own valour but also of that of the unnamed officers and men of a very gallant ship's company, many of whom have not returned.

Captured during the raid, he was released from captivity at the end of the war. He later achieved the rank of captain, before being appointed, in 1965, naval attaché to Ethiopia, where he was awarded the Order of Menelik II. Also the recipient of the French Legion d'Honneur and the Croix de Guerre avec Palmes, he died aged 67, on April 20, 1975, in Cornwall.

In addition to the crew, each motorboat in the flotilla carried about 15 commandos. During the first part of the crossing, the commandos had to stay hidden inside the boats so as not to attract the attention of Luftwaffe reconnaissance planes. (The National Archives)

The Flotilla Sails to Warmer Seas

On Thursday, March 26, in the early afternoon, the *Chariot* flotilla left Falmouth. The crews were dressed in tropical outfits and colonial helmets—a disguise designed to deceive the ever-watchful Germans as to their true destination for as long as possible.

At 1400 on Thursday, March 26, 1942, the motorboat flotilla set sail from the port of Falmouth, escorted by an RAF fighter flying at low altitude. An hour later, it was the turn of *Campbeltown* and the two escort destroyers to weigh anchor. Newman and Ryder boarded the *Atherstone* with their staffs. Initially scheduled to begin on March 27, the operation was advanced by one day at Ryder's request due to deteriorating weather conditions.

Once assembled, the flotilla sailed southwest at a speed of 14 knots. It consisted of 611 men: 345 sailors, 257 commandos (166 assault troops and 91 demolition crew), a medical team of four, two journalists sent by the Ministry of Information, and three liaison officers.

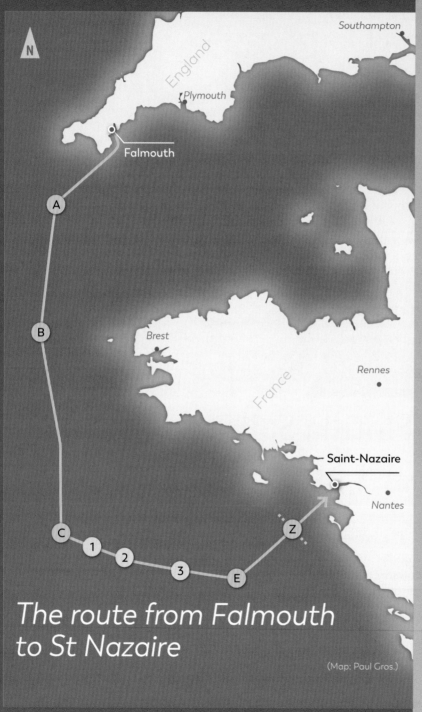

The route from Falmouth to St Nazaire

(Map: Paul Gros.)

A Thursday, March 26, 1910: The flotilla is located southwest of the Scilly Isles. Having reached point "A," it heads south. Ryder orders the flotilla to adopt a crescent formation for the night. The speed is 14 knots. The air escort departs.

B Thursday, March 26, 2300: The flotilla enters enemy waters, where it is likely to cross paths with U-boats transiting between their bases in Brest, Lorient, St Nazaire, and the Atlantic, on the hunt for Allied cargo ships. It is now also in range of German aircraft stationed in northern Brittany.

C Friday, March 27, 0700: The flotilla is 260 kilometers from St Nazaire. After reaching point "C," it changes course to 112° and reduces its speed to 8 knots.

E Friday, March 27, 2000: At point "E," the fleet stops. Ryder and Newman are transferred from the *Atherstone* to the MGB *314*, which will serve as their command post for the attack. It heads north towards the Loire estuary at a speed of 15 knots.

Z Friday, March 27, 2215: The flotilla reaches the rendezvous point with the submarine *Sturgeon*, positioned at point "Z." The *Atherstone* and *Tynedale* leave *Campbeltown* and the motorboats, now only 75 kilometers from their final destination.

1 Friday, March 27, 0720: The *Tynedale* spots a German submarine (*U-593*) cruising about 10 kilometers from the flotilla. The two escort destroyers approach and engage in combat.

2 Friday, March 27, 1200: One then several French trawlers are spotted. Ryder gives the order to sink two of them after collecting their crews.

3 Friday, March 27, 2005: ML *10* has engine problems, so its commandos are transferred to ML *15*, the reserve motorboat.

Commander Robert Ryder, commander-in-chief of the flotilla. (The National Archives)

Among them was a Frenchman: Lieutenant Jack William Lee (22), aka Raymond Couraud, was in charge of making contact with the Nazairians at the time of the landing to facilitate the operation and limit civilian losses. Lieutenant Stuart Chant, who had worked on the London Stock Exchange before the war, was traveling on the *Campbeltown*. He later remembered that, as the ships got underway, he and his comrades felt a sense of relief to be on their way to their destination. They were also under no illusions that their chances of returning to the land now disappearing over the horizon were slim at best.

The *Atherstone* led the way, towing MGB *314*. Next were the *Tynedale* and *Campbeltown*, the latter towing Micky Wynn's MTB *74*. The motorboats carrying the commandos sailed in two parallel columns flanking the destroyers, following each other at an interval of 200 meters. To facilitate their identification, each had a number painted on its funnel, from 1 to 16. Subject to a strict radio silence, the *Chariot* vessels were only able to communicate using visual signals.

Any German aviator who risked flying over the flotilla would not spot a single man in commando uniform on the *Campbeltown* or its motorboat entourage. All he would see were sailors in waxed duffle coats or light-colored turtleneck sweaters on bridges cluttered with colonial helmets and tropical clothing. In short, nothing out of the ordinary for the sailors of the "10th Antisubmarine Strike Force," a dummy unit ostensibly formed to hunt U-boats in warmer seas, from the Bay of Biscay to the Suez Canal. To make the disguise even more convincing, the boats were accompanied by a Bristol Beaufighter, a twin-engined aircraft to torpedo- or rocket-based attacks on enemy shipping.

Shortly after 1900, the convoy, having reached point "A" of its route, southeast of the Scilly Isles, received Ryder's order to head south. The air escort returned to base, as the flotilla found itself facing a long night of navigational challenges.

Lieutenant-Commander Stephen "Sam" Beattie, commander of the *Campbeltown*. (The National Archives)

The weather was superb at dawn on Friday, March 27, when the flotilla reached point "C," some 250 kilometers west of St Nazaire. This did not please Ryder, who would have preferred some cloud cover while approaching the target. The commander-in-chief had good reason to be wary. Two days earlier, study of the latest aerial photos of St Nazaire revealed the presence of five German torpedo boats that had not previously been spotted. The Wolf- and Möwe-class vessels were fast and well-armed, and posed a serious threat to the operation.

According to the operational schedule, Ryder set course to 112° and reduced speed to 8 knots. The *Campbeltown* and two escort destroyers hoisted the Kriegsmarine ensign to deceive the Luftwaffe. A few minutes later, shortly before 0730, the *Tynedale*'s officer of the watch reported a suspicious vessel, which could be either a fishing boat or a submarine, about 10 kilometers to port. Shortly afterward, the *Tynedale* lookout confirmed that it was a submarine surfacing. The *Tynedale* headed full speed toward the U-boat, followed by the *Atherstone*, which cut MTB 74 loose. The submarine sent a light signal to the *Tynedale*, which was still flying the German flag. The latter responded in kind, continuing to advance.

When it was about 5 kilometers from the submarine, the *Tynedale* hauled down its German colors and hoisted the White Ensign, the flag of the Royal Navy, and opened fire. The U-boat dived immediately. The destroyer reacted by launching depth charges, the detonations forcing the submarine to the surface. A new and even more ferocious salvo forced the U-boat to dive again, this time for good.

Fearing that the U-boat had seen the rest of the flotilla and had time to signal its presence, Ryder ordered the destroyers to follow it. Both tried to depth-charge the submarine but failed, the *Tynedale* having lost the use of its antisubmarine detection system during the scuffle. Finally, Ryder ordered the destroyers to rejoin the flotilla, but heading southwest to mislead the German submarine in case it had not sunk.

Shortly before noon, the flotilla spotted several trawlers. Knowing that the Germans placed radio observers on French fishing vessels, Ryder decided to sink two of the boats that were clearly separated from the group—the *Nungesser and Coli* and *La Slack*—after capturing their crews. Finding nothing suspicious on the two boats, Ryder gave the order to leave the rest of the trawlers alone.

In the early afternoon, as the British flotilla continued its journey eastward, the German garrison at St Nazaire was hosting a distinguished guest. Having arrived to inspect the expansion of the base, Admiral Karl Dönitz decided to take advantage of the trip to celebrate the return of two U-boats: *U-87*, back from a long surveillance mission off the Norwegian coast; and *U-588*, which had sunk four enemy ships off the North American coast between January 22 and March 10.

After having greeted the crews and inspected the 10 resident submarines, Dönitz and the officers proceeded to La Baule, where a reception had been organized. Here, the Grand Admiral asked Lieutenant-Commander Herbert Sohler, commander of the 7th U-boat Flotilla, what he would do if the British came to St Nazaire.

Dönitz had not asked this question by chance. According to the latest report sent to his headquarters, the British had chosen St Nazaire to test the destructive power of their new bombs before launching raids against other port facilities in France and the rest of occupied Europe.

Unfazed, Sohler replied that it was absolutely unthinkable that any enemy could enter the port, taking care to point out that the only passage deep enough to reach St Nazaire,

HMS *Atherstone* was the flotilla's second escort vessel. Like HMS *Tynedale*, it was a Hunt-class destroyer, and was launched in December 1939. In late 1941, it was transferred to the Devonport-based 15th Destroyer Flotilla, in Plymouth harbor. During Operation *Chariot*, it served as Newman's and Ryder's command post as far as the Loire estuary. The *Atherstone* served in the Royal Navy until the mid-1950s. (Imperial War Museum)

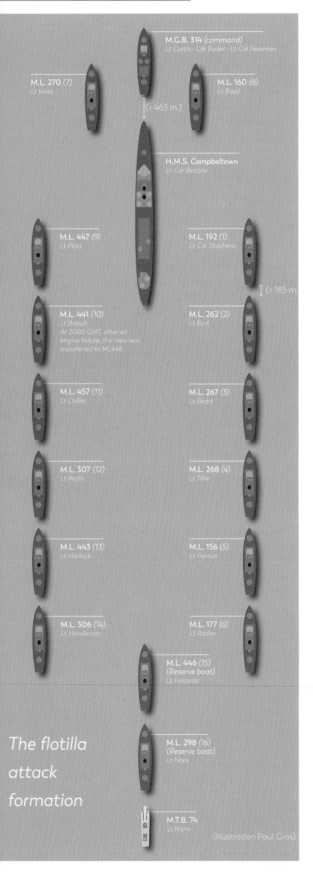

M.G.B. 314 (command)
Lt Curtis - Cdr Ryder - Lt-Col Newman

M.L. 270 (7)
Lt Irwin

M.L. 160 (8)
Lt Boyd

(≈ 463 m.)

H.M.S. Campbeltown
Lt-Cdr Beattie

M.L. 447 (9)
Lt Platt

M.L. 192 (1)
Lt-Cdr Stephens

(≈ 185 m.)

M.L. 441 (10)
Lt Briault
At 2000 GMT, after an
engine failure, the crew was
transferred to ML446

M.L. 262 (2)
Lt Burt

M.L. 457 (11)
Lt Collier

M.L. 267 (3)
Lt Beart

M.L. 307 (12)
Lt Wallis

M.L. 268 (4)
Lt Tillie

M.L. 443 (13)
Lt Horlock

M.L. 156 (5)
Lt Fenton

M.L. 306 (14)
Lt Henderson

M.L. 177 (6)
Lt Radier

M.L. 446 (15)
(Reserve boat)
Lt Falconar

The flotilla

attack

formation

M.L. 298 (16)
(Reserve boat)
Lt Nock

M.T.B. 74
Lt Wynn

(Illustration Paul Gros)

namely the Charpentiers Channel, was directly in the line of fire of several powerful batteries of the 280th Naval Artillery Battalion.

Dönitz's reply left everyone present, not least Sohler himself, perplexed: "In your position, I would not be so confident."

And yet, the commander-in-chief of the German submarine fleet ignored a message transmitted by *U-593* earlier that afternoon. The U-boat in question had remained submerged for over five hours after its encounter with the *Tynedale* and the *Atherstone*, and transmitted the following message once it resurfaced: "0620 [German time]. Three destroyers and ten speedboats at 46°52'N and 48°W. Heading west."

According to the headings reported by *U-593*, the staff of Marine Group Command West inferred that the identified enemy ships were conducting a mine-laying operation or else heading toward Gibraltar. As a precaution, they transmitted the information to the Luftwaffe, as well as to the commanders of the Naval Protection Force and ordered the five torpedo boats—those spotted by RAF reconnaissance aircraft two days earlier at St Nazaire and subsequently regrouped at Nantes—to leave the estuary on a reconnaissance mission.

As Dönitz's car drove toward Lorient, the British flotilla continued on its way without encountering any major obstacles. The only problem that befell the flotilla that afternoon was the failure of ML*10*'s one engine; the commandos on board were transferred to ML*15*, one of the reserve motorboats. When he received a report of five German torpedo boats sighted off St Nazaire, shortly after 1700, Ryder decided to reinforce security for the

Britsh Order of Battle

ROYAL NAVY

HMS *Campbeltown*

HMS *Tynedale*

HMS *Atherstone*

HMS *Sturgeon*

Motor Gun Boat 314

Motor Torpedo Boat 74

28th Motor Launch Flotilla

7th Motor Launch Flotilla

20th Motor Launch Flotilla

BRITISH ARMY

No. 2 Commando

Special Service Brigade (part)

ROYAL AIR FORCE

No. 51 Squadron

No. 58 Squadron

No. 77 Squadron

No. 103 Squadron

No. 150 Squadron

entire flotilla. To reduce the risk of identification, he ordered the boats to limit their light signals and to cover the windows of the gangways with grease, paint, or paper.

Despite the threat, the men on board remained in good spirits. On the *Campbeltown*, Captain Donald Roy's Scots, recognizable as much by their taste for singing and fighting as by their kilts, seemed in particularly good humor. In addition to sunglasses, colonial helmets and tropical shirts, the old destroyer was full of food that delighted the commandos: eggs, sausages, ham, butter, cereal bars, cakes, milk, tea, hot chocolate, and, of course, cartons of cigarettes. Some jokers went so far as to make soap and toothpaste sandwiches, with the idea that the Germans boarding the *Campbeltown* at St Nazaire might sample the "feast."

The second day at sea ended without incident. ML*15* finally rejoined the flotilla, having fallen behind to rescue the commandos stranded on ML*10*. The latter was forced to return to England on a single functioning engine, and took no further part in the operation.

Under a heavy cloud cover, ideal for concealment, the flotilla advanced slowly so that the bows of the boats produced as little white water as possible. There was no sign of enemy aircraft overhead. The Admiralty forwarded Ryder a message from Plymouth, stating that the five German torpedo boats sighted the previous day had been observed returning to St Nazaire.

At 2000, the flotilla arrived at point "E" of its route. There, it changed course again and turned northeast. The boats then paused to adopt attack formation. The *Campbeltown* hooked up with Micky Wynn's MTB *74*, and the *Atherstone* did likewise with MGB *314*. Before boarding the motorboat that would serve as their command post for the final phase of the crossing, Newman, Ryder and their staffs received warm wishes and encouragement from Lieutenant-Commander Robert "Jumbo" Jenks, commander of the *Atherstone*, and his crew gathered on deck. While the transfer went well for Ryder and Newman, the same could not be said for Stanley Day, who misjudged his jump from the destroyer and got his leg stuck between the hulls of the two boats.

In Profile:
Fairmile B Motor Launch and Fairmile C MGB *314*

Fairmile B Motor Launch: 16 of these were used in Operation *Chariot*.

Fairmile C Motor Gun Boat 314: Charles Newman's and Robert Ryder's command boat during the raid on St Nazaire.

Technical specifications

Built entirely of wood
Length: 34.5 meters (113 ft 4 in)
Width/beam: 5.5 meters (18 feet)
Displacement: 90 tons
Propulsion: 2 × gasoline engines, 12 × Hall Scott cylinders (850hp)
Maximum speed: 20 knots
Armament: 1 × 20mm Oerlikon or 40mm Bofors gun in the bow,
   1 × 20mm Oerlikon gun at the stern, 2 × 7.7mm double Lewis
   machine-gun positions behind the bridge. Some also carried
   antisubmarine depth charges or torpedoes.
In addition to the initial crew of 15 (including two officers), each
   boat carried sailors specializing in weapons, mechanics, radio, and
   navigation.

(Thierry Vallet)

Technical specifications

Built entirely of wood
Length: 33.5 meters (110 ft)
Width/beam: 5 meters (16 ft 5 in)
Displacement: 70 tons
Propulsion: 3 × gasoline engines, 12 × cylinders (650hp)
Maximum speed: 26 knots
Armament: 1 × 4mm Vickers "pom-pom" gun at the bow, 2 × 12.7mm
   machine guns amidship, 1 × 47mm Rolls Royce automatic gun at the
   stern.
For Operation *Chariot*, this motorboat also had its initial crew of about
   15 supplemented with several specialized sailors.

(Thierry Vallet)

With MGB *314* in the lead, followed at 450 meters by the *Campbeltown*, flanked by the motorboats in two columns, and with Micky Wynn's "customized" vessel bringing up the rear, the flotilla closed in on the estuary at a speed of 12 knots. They still had about 100 kilometers to go.

Thanks in part to the extraordinary level-headedness he had displayed since leaving Falmouth, Lieutenant-Commander Bill Green had directed the flotilla with astonishing precision over some 700 kilometers on the high seas. In fact, he led the convoy precisely to the light signal from the *Sturgeon* submarine, positioned as a beacon at point "Z", 75 kilometers from the French coast. The final point of reference before the estuary, the submarine had been transmitting the letter "M" out toward the open sea for about 22 hours.

As the MGB *314* passed the half-submerged *Sturgeon*, Ryder, loudspeaker in hand, thanked Commander Mervyn Wingfield, who was standing on the turret. The submarine commander shouted back: "Goodbye and good luck, lads!"

The *Atherstone*'s and *Tynedale*'s journey stopped here; the *Campbeltown* and motorboats would proceed without them to their final destination. But the destroyers' mission was not over yet: the two brave "guard dogs" would continue patrolling outside the estuary until the return of the flotilla, scheduled for the next day.

As for the *Sturgeon*, which had completed its mission perfectly, it dived and left no sign it had ever been there.

The 611 commandos and sailors of Operation *Chariot* were now alone in the night. Behind them was the open sea, ahead the fearsome estuary, littered with shoals and riddled with gun emplacements.

At 2300 on Friday, March 27, Nigel Tibbits, assisted by a sailor, primed the *Campbeltown*'s time-delayed rockets. As the acid began to gnaw away at the copper, it became clear to all that there was now no turning back. The explosion was imminent, but the question remained as to when exactly it would happen. The five tons of explosives positioned at the front of the destroyer were due to detonate after eight hours. But taking into account a significant margin of error, the "fireworks" could begin any time between 0500 and 0900.

Aboard MGB *314*, Ryder and Newman were more vigilant than ever, on the lookout for any noise or suspicious movement. The palpable tension was in stark contrast to Bill Green's relaxed attitude. When he was not busy making calculations in his small navigation station, he was on deck looking at the night sky and joking with the men at his side. As on the other motorboats, sailors manning the armaments stood to at their guns and machine guns.

From time to time, Ryder glanced behind him to make sure the other vessels, which stretched for over a kilometer, were proceeding smoothly. The commander was delighted when it started to drizzle, the light rain forming a protective curtain around the flotilla.

At 2330, while the flotilla was still offshore, the men on board the motorboats and the *Campbeltown* heard the drone of Wellington and Whitley bombers overhead. From their vessels, they saw the beams of the searchlights scanning the low sky and the gleam of enemy Flak, and heard the sound of bombs exploding in the distance. The battle for St Nazaire had begun.

After 30 hours of zigzagging across the English Channel to deceive the Germans, Newman's commandos were ready to activate their stiff muscles.

HMS *Campbeltown* Hits the Bullseye

In spite of the increasingly intense fire from the Germans on the approach to St Nazaire, the *Campbeltown* succeeding in opening up the Joubert lock according to plan. But for the commandos, the hard part was about to begin.

The arrival of enemy bombers overhead led the commander of the St Nazaire antiaircraft defenses to sound the *flieger alarm* (air-raid alert) from his command post at Saint-Marc, at the western entrance of the estuary. But the more he watched the sky, the more confused naval Captain Karl-Conrad Mecke became: the RAF aircraft were dropping significantly fewer bombs than in previous raids. In the spirit of better safe than sorry, Mecke dispatched patrols just in case paratroopers were being dropped.

The RAF's unusual behavior was also noted by the St Nazaire residents. "Usually the bombs come straight after the air raid siren sounds, but this time it was strange. The aircraft

The *Campbeltown* succeeded in embedding itself in the outer caisson of the Joubert lock, only four minutes behind schedule. On the deck are the ladders used by the commandos to disembark. (Bundesarchiv)

The port of St Nazaire, seen from the south, with the outer harbor in the foreground. On the right is the Old Mole jetty and its two concrete casemates, while the Joubert lock is a little farther north. (The National Archives)

were circling but nothing was happening. Everyone said to themselves: 'It's not normal, it's not like the other times,'" observed Michèle Morisseau, a child at the time, whose father, a member of the Civil Defense, ran a brewery near the port that doubled as an air-raid shelter for 200 people.

The flotilla entered the estuary at 0030. Its fate rested heavily on the shoulders of one man: Lieutenant-Commander Bill Green. He had the formidable task of steering the *Campbeltown* through the shoals. Twice, the old destroyer scraped along sandbanks, but he did not falter and kept steaming ahead, regardless.

On board the boats, the men took up combat positions, while reserve tanks were filled with seawater in anticipation of fires. On the *Campbeltown*, Major Copland issued his final instructions to the team. The commandos lay in the center of the boat, sheltered behind the armored barriers, their weapons and explosive charges pressed tightly against their bodies. Sam Beattie and Nigel Tibbits stood on the bridge.

The flotilla was now less than 10 kilometers from St Nazaire, in attack formation, with the *Campbeltown* surrounded by motorboats and the commanders' MGB *314* in the center. There was a strange, even surreal calm aboard the various boats. Like Newman and Ryder, sailors and commandos could hardly believe the absence of an enemy reaction, and enjoyed the reassuring roar of the RAF bombers overhead.

"Looks like someone on the ground is keeping the Germans' eyes sealed so they don't see us coming," said Newman to Ryder, as they stood inside MGB *314*'s cockpit.

"It's almost too good to be true," Ryder thought out loud as the convoy passed to the port side of the Morées Tower, which stood in the middle of the estuary, about 2.5 kilometers from the harbor entrance and 3 kilometers from the Joubert lock.

A few seconds later, as if to answer the two *Chariot* commanders, searchlights lit up on the northern bank and illuminated the estuary.

It was 0102.

Sweeping the estuary with his binoculars from his command post at Saint-Brevin, Lieutenant-Commander Lothar Burhenne, commander of the 809th German Marine Artillery Group, had just spotted the flotilla sailing at full speed, lights out, straight toward St Nazaire.

Soon, beams from both shores swept the waters of the estuary and finally revealed the two long columns of motorboats and the German-style torpedo ship flying the flag of the Third Reich, guns pointed skyward as if to open fire on enemy aircraft.

The bow of the *Campbeltown* embedded in the outer caisson of the Joubert lock. German soldiers have boarded to inspect it. (St Nazaire Ecomuseum)

The German lookouts immediately began interrogating these unknown vessels with light signals, while flurries of gunfire came from artillery batteries on the Villès-Martin point. Ryder increased the speed to 19 knots and instructed Quartermaster Signalman Seymour Pike to send a message to all vessels in the flotilla: "Fire only when I give the order."

Disguised as a Kriegsmarine petty officer, standing on the gangway of MGB *314*, Pike then emitted the German reconnaissance signal with his lamp, a skill he had learned from the transmissions book stolen during the Norway operations. Next, by means of the same code, he transmitted the following message to the Germans:

"Urgent. I am escorting two damaged ships to port. Requesting entry."

The ploy earned the convoy a few precious minutes, but the artillery fire soon resumed.

Ryder gave Pike a new order, to transmit a new message to the Germans: "You are firing on friendly forces."

The gunfire ceased again, but this time, it was too late. Alerted by a lookout announcing the approach of a group of boats, Captain Mecke had already sounded warning of a potential enemy landing. This had the immediate effect of directing all antiaircraft batteries toward the estuary and activating all available troops, as well as the crews of the various vessels docked in the port.

At 0128, with the flotilla less than 2 kilometers from port, the coastal floodlights suddenly lit up again and the artillery barrage resumed. Ryder ordered all his ships to open fire in response, but their light weapons were ineffective against the coastal batteries of 75mm, 150mm, and 170mm guns. The most powerful weapon the British flotilla had was the 76.2mm gun mounted at the bow of the *Campbeltown*.

This photo of the bow of *Campbeltown* shows the damage caused by German shelling. (Bundesarchiv)

This photo shows how *Campbeltown's* stern was submerged. One of its two funnels is still smoking, and the damage caused by shells is visible on the hull. In the background are the cranes in the harbor area, and the concrete building whose rooftop guns were neutralized by Lieutenant Roderick's commandos as they disembarked the *Campbeltown.* (Bundesarchiv)

Despite the inferiority of their weapons, the British gunners somehow managed to silence a few batteries. Surprisingly, none of the motorboats was sunk during these first minutes of the fierce German bombardment. In his report, Ryder noted that it was hard to imagine the intensity of fire on both sides.

Right from the beginning of the artillery barrage, it was on the *Campbeltown,* illuminated by the searchlights located on both sides of the estuary, that most of the enemy fire was directed. Sitting in the officers' quarters, Lieutenant Corran Purdon, leader of the commando team tasked with destroying the Normandie Dock's inner caisson operating system, heard the shells slamming against the hull; he even saw one cross the cabin and emerge without exploding.

From the bridge, Beattie gave the order the push the *Campbeltown* harder, faster, knowing that it needed to reach a speed of 20 knots in order to ram the outer caisson, which was over 10 meters thick and the same height as a six-story building. Unperturbed by the enemy fire, he gave constant course adjustments while his eight Oerlikons and his 76.2mm gun pounded the German coastal defenses. Around him, the bridge was covered with dead and wounded. A shell had killed the helmsman instantly; he was immediately replaced.

As the convoy approached the port, the battle became increasingly violent. Shells and bullets impacted the destroyer from all angles, tearing armor plate, piercing bulkheads,

The concrete building located to the east of the Joubert lock's outer caisson. Lieutenant Roderick's commandos reached the roof using the stairs at the rear of the building, then neutralized the guns positioned there. (The National Archives)

killing and injuring sailors and commandos alike. As the bridge was now too exposed, Beattie brought as many men as he could down into the navigation station, protected from small-arms fire by its armor plating. It was just as well he did, as a large-caliber shell hit the 76.2mm gun with full force, killing the gunners and destroying the mortars arranged at the bow of the ship.

Realizing that the *Campbeltown* was too far to port, Beattie ordered Tibbits to turn to starboard. As Beattie searched for a point of reference with his binoculars, a German searchlight picked out the lighthouse at the end of the Old Mole. Thanks to this unexpected revelation, the commander of *Campbeltown* got his bearings and was able to direct the convoy straight toward to the caisson, now less than a kilometer away.

The command motorboat led the way and then, as planned, veered off to starboard at full speed. Leaving the Southern Entrance to port, the destroyer sped forward with all its power, straight at the Joubert lock, framed by the Old Mole and fuel tanks of the East Zone.

"Brace for impact!" exclaimed Beattie.

The commandos clung to anything they could, their weapons and explosive charges tight against them, feet well forward to protect their heads from the imminent shock. All around and above them was hell. Every cannon and machine gun in the port area was firing on the old destroyer, claiming further casualties on the devastated bridge, already strewn with the dead and dying.

Less than 200 meters from the target, Beattie finally made out the huge black shape of the metal caisson, standing out against the illuminated sky streaked by the searchlights. At the last moment, he ordered the helmsman to turn 20° to port, so as to hit the caisson dead-center and to avoid blocking the opening of the Old Entrance for the motorboats.

In a dreadful tearing of metal and shower of sparks, the *Campbeltown* struck the caisson with such force that its bow plunged more than 10 meters into the lock. Despite the violence of the impact, most of the men were not too badly shaken.

Solidly implanted in the caisson, the *Campbeltown*'s bow was angled upward at 20°, while the stern was practically submerged.

"Well, here we are, four minutes late," Beattie said quietly, looking at his watch.

It was indeed 0134 GMT, on March 28, 1942.

***

The first phase of the operation, the most important and the most delicate of all, had just been successfully completed. Quickly shooting down the guards on the two fuel tankers in the Joubert dry dock, the *Passat* and the *Schlettstadt*, the commandos rushed toward the score of objectives they had to destroy before sunrise, one against ten.

The assault troops were the first to leave the *Campbeltown*, those under the command of Lieutenant John Roderick on the starboard side and those under Captain Roy on the port side. These men had to silence four guns, eliminate the guards of the underground fuel tanks and, if possible, throw incendiary grenades into the ventilation ducts of these tanks.

Within 20 minutes, Roderick's group had completed its mission, and, despite being outnumbered by the defenders, had killed several Germans and reduced their number to no more than a dozen. But the arrival of German reinforcements made it increasingly difficult to defend the perimeter and provide cover for the demolition teams operating at the end of the Joubert lock, beside the Penhoët basin.

The Joubert-style pumping station, whose defenses were neutralized by Captain Donald Roy's Scots, is still standing today. (J-C Stasi)

Faced with ever-increasing enemy troops, Roderick's commandos finally retreated after about 40 minutes, in the mistaken belief that Newman had launched the green flare, giving the order to fall back. To return to the boats, the commandos had to cross the outer caisson again, and, as the bow of *Campbeltown* was blocking the way, they had to climb onto the old destroyer again to reach the other side, picking their way through the corpses and the debris littering the devastated deck.

Captain Roy, who had been deprived of his second-in-command, Lieutenant John Proctor, who was seriously wounded on board the *Campbeltown*, had a similar mission to Roderick's, but on the other side of the Joubert lock. His group's first objective was the artillery battery positioned on the roof of the pumping station, just a few meters from the outer caisson on the left side of the dry dock. The commandos accessed the battery using the external staircase located at the rear of the building, and placed their charges in the breeches of the two guns. No sooner had they descended again than the charges exploded, showering them with rubble and debris.

The next task was to hold the bridge over the Old Entrance, southwest of the pumping station, to allow the demolition teams to withdraw to the Old Mole jetty where reembarkation would take place. As soon as they arrived in the vicinity, the Scots were subjected to heavy fire from the German guns on the other side of the basin, as well as incoming artillery fire from the vessels moored in the basin, not to mention German infantrymen converging on them from the port area. Like Roderick, Roy had fulfilled his mission, but at a price: half of his men were casualties.

Private Tom McCormack, a member of Captain Roy's assault group. Seriously wounded in the face and right arm, he died two weeks after the raid, at the military hospital in Rennes. He was 25 years old. His image was used widely by German propaganda, and became a symbol of the British commandos' defeat. (Bundesarchiv)

Private Tom McCormack being lifted onto a flatbed truck by his captors. (Bundesarchiv)

Alongside Lance-Sergeants King, Arthur Dockerill, Ronald Butler, and Cyril Chamberlain, Lieutenant Stuart Chant of the Gordon Highlanders was tasked with the destruction of the Joubert-style pumping station. Unfortunately, he was seriously injured by German shelling just before the *Campbeltown* hit its mark, as was Chamberlain. But shrapnel in his knee, arm and hands did not prevent him from leading his men.

Weighed down by their explosive charges, incendiary devices, mallets and axes, Chant and his commandos hit their first obstacle when they arrived outside the pumping station: they had planned for everything—except the heavy metal door being locked. Luckily, Captain Montgomery solved the unforeseen problem with a small magnetic charge.

Once inside, the commandos used their powerful flashlights to quickly locate the staircase leading to the pump room. Chamberlain was becoming weaker, so Chant decided to leave him at the foot of the stairs to stand guard. Thus, only four men instead of five began the spiral staircase.

Chant in the lead, the commandos descended, each holding onto the backpack of the man in front of him. Once in the basement, the team headed to one of the four large pumps used to drain the lock. As they had practiced dozens of times in training, the four demolitions men placed their heavy backpacks on the ground and took out their explosive charges: eight per pump, specially prepared, waterproofed and double-wired, amounting to more than 18 pounds of explosives per pump. As planned, the commandos placed the charges on the parts of the pumps that were the most difficult to replace, to keep the pumping station out of action for as long as possible.

Captured, Lieutenant Roderick (center) and his commandos are held on board a German minesweeper moored in front of the submarine base. (Bundesarchiv)

With all charges placed, the commandos proceeded to connect up the system, filling the two detonating cords with the prepared primers. Once the striker was activated, they had just 90 seconds to escape before the explosion.

Back in the open, Chant and his men crouched behind a protective wall. Suddenly Captain Montgomery appeared, shouting at them to get farther away from the station. And he was right to do so: the tremendous explosion as 80 kilograms of plastic explosives threw debris out at great force over dozens of meters all around, destroying the wall the commandos had been sheltering behind seconds before.

While Chant and his sergeants were working 12 meters underground, Lieutenant Christopher Smalley's team destroyed the outer caisson's operating station, just a few meters from the pumping station.

Lieutenant Gerard Brett, a conservation assistant at the Victoria and Albert Museum in London, led a team whose target was the inner caisson of the Joubert lock. Another group, led by Lieutenant Robert Burtenshaw, initially responsible for destroying the outer caisson should the *Campbeltown* fail, acted as reinforcements to help Brett accomplish his risky mission. Burtenshaw was hard to miss: he was a giant of a man, who always wore a monocle and disembarked the boat singing, waving a cane and wearing—for some unknown reason— naval officer Sam Beattie's cap.

The reinforcements soon proved valuable. Indeed, Brett was seriously wounded in the legs and an arm as he ran across the 400 meters of exposed ground to the inner caisson; he had to be left behind the shelter of a wall. Galvanized by Burtenshaw, who continued to sing as if nothing were remiss, the commandos from the two groups merged into a single force and began to work. Under the direction of Sergeant Frank Carr, they lowered 12 explosive charges, each weighing 8 kilograms, down the northern side of the caisson—the one facing the Penhoët basin—until they were below water level, before attaching the suspension ropes to the railing. After that, they assembled the firing system, arranging the fuses and detonators.

Meanwhile, Burtenshaw, with the help of Sergeant Stewart Deery, was attempting to open the panel giving access to the interior of the caisson, into which they had to lower the rest of the charges. Frustrated with his lack of progress, Burtenshaw resorted to the use of explosives, but still could not force open the panel. The noise he was making attracted the attention of the Germans, who then concentrated their fire on Burtenshaw and his men. Artillery and machine-gun fired rained down on them from emplacements to the left of the caisson, as German troops and sailors began arriving from the station area and the vessels moored in the Penhoët basin. The crews of the nearest two oil tankers being repaired in the dry dock strafed the commandos from close range using all available weapons.

Burtenshaw quickly realized that he and his men would not be able to escape if they did not do something immediately. He ordered an assault on the tanker, even though his demolition teams had only their Colt .45s against the artillery pieces and machine guns of the enemy sailors. Fortunately, they were able to rely on the reinforcements provided by Lieutenant Mallinson "Bung" Denison who had been defending the caisson. But the commandos were taken by surprise by a fresh group of Germans, who attacked them from the rear. Already wounded, Burtenshaw managed to shoot down several assailants before he himself was killed. One of his corporals, Arthur Blount, was also killed in the engagement.

With Brett and Burtenshaw out of action, Sergeant Carr immediately took control of operations and climbed back onto the inner caisson. After activating the 12 submerged charges, he had 60 seconds to escape from the caisson and find shelter. The sound of water from the Penhoët basin rushing and bubbling into the Joubert lock heralded his success.

The submarine base today, seen from the Old Entrance lock. (J-C Stasi)

With the inner caisson ruined, Lieutenant Purdon's group of four commandos were now able to blow up its operating station. Purdon, a 21-year-old Irish veteran of the Norway operations, initiated the detonation. More than 70 years later, as a retired general, Corran Purdon still remembered the spectacle caused by the tremendous explosion: "The whole building seemed to rise up several feet, before falling apart into a pile of rubble, like a pack of cards."

On the water, the motorboats were facing strong resistance from the Germans. Motorboat Group 1 had to land at the Old Mole. The 200-meter-long jetty with a lighthouse at the end was by far the more dangerous of the two berths. Indeed, exposed to fire from artillery batteries positioned on both sides, the Old Mole was also strongly defended by two concrete casements, one in the middle and the other just before the lighthouse. The first was equipped with a 20mm gun and the second with a powerful searchlight.

The first Group 1 motorboat to arrive was Lieutenant Thomas Platt's ML *9*. It carried Captain David Birney's assault group, who were responsible for neutralizing the defenses of the Old Mole jetty, then securing the area between the jetty and the Southern Entrance of the St Nazaire basin.

When it was still about 10 meters from the Old Mole, ML *9* was hit by enemy fire. The boat attempted to moor but ran aground a few meters from its mark. Heavily strafed and showered with grenades, ML *9* managed to escape, but had caught fire and carried many dead and wounded. The sailors and commandos who were physically capable of doing so finally jumped into the water to try to swim to shore. Captain Birney managed to reach it, but died of cold and exhaustion a few hours later.

Behind Platt's boat came naval Lieutenant Thomas Collier's ML *11*, carrying Captain Pritchard, responsible for all the destruction in the New Entrance area; then Lieutenant

Explosives abandoned by British commandos. (Bundesarchiv)

A dead British commando. (Bundesarchiv)

Walton's demolition team, responsible for destroying the bridge and lock gates at the northern end of the New Entrance; and finally, the protection squad led by the very young Lieutenant Watson, nicknamed "Tiger."

After narrowly avoiding the fleeing ML 9, Collier managed to get all his passengers off his boat and down the long slipway. About half an hour later, however, as it withdrew to the middle of the estuary, waiting for the reembarkation signal, ML 11 was hit by several shells and exploded, killing half the crew, including Lieutenant Collier.

Just behind Collier's boat, Australian Lieutenant Norman Wallis's ML 12 was carrying Captain Richard Bradley's team, tasked with destroying the central lock gate at the Southern Entrance. Having missed the slipway due to heavy enemy fire, it attempted to reach the Old Mole on the other side. Unfortunately, the water was shallow, and ML 12 ran aground before it could withdraw for a second attempt. When it tried to berth for a third time, ML 12 suffered such an intense barrage of enemy fire that it had to abandon its attempts to land its commandos.

The next three boats, ML 13, ML 14 and ML 15, were equally unsuccessful. With each new attempt to berth, the boats were forced to retreat by shells, bullets and grenades. Finally, they were ordered to return to the high seas, much to the frustration of the commandos on board, some of whom were shot or otherwise wounded before they even had a chance to fight. On board ML 15, Captain Hodgson, commander of an assault group, was killed and two of his men seriously wounded.

Within five minutes of *Campbeltown*'s impact in the Joubert dock, only one of six motorboats had managed to land its commandos at the Old Mole: the one carrying Captain Pritchard, Lieutenant Walton's demolition team and Lieutenant Watson. All the men who had been unable to disembark were sorely missed in the coming hours by their comrades in the harbor and the old town.

Four hundred meters farther north, the Old Entrance was the designated landing point for two columns of motorboats carrying the commandos of Group 2. Lieutenant-

The Germans fortified the Old Mole jetty with two concrete casements, the first equipped with a 20mm gun and the second with a powerful searchlight that considerably hindered the approach of British motorboats that were to berth at the jetty. (Paul Gros)

The Old Mole today, seen from the same angle. (Hubert Chemereau)

Commander William Stephens's ML *1* carried Captain Michael Burn, leader of Group 2, and the dozen men from Lieutenant Peyton's assault team, tasked with attacking the swing bridge at the northern end of the Joubert lock and neutralizing the guns located between the St Nazaire basin and the Penhoët basin.

Aged 30, Michael Burn was an unusual character, as phlegmatic as he was nonconformist. Poet, writer, and journalist, he had been fascinated during the mid-1930s—as with many other Britons—by the splendor of the Nazi "mass rallies", to the point of being dedicated a copy of *Mein Kampf* by the Führer himself during a stay in Munich. But his fascination with the Third Reich did not prevent him from joining the independent companies, which gave birth to the first commandos, as soon as war was declared.

Hit by several shells which caused irreparable damage to its machinery, ML *1* crossed the port-side column and crashed on the east pier, two hundred meters south of the Old Mole jetty. But with the wharf more than four meters above them, it was impossible for the survivors to disembark. The wounded were placed on the inflatable life rafts while the uninjured jumped into the water, Captain Burn among them. Successfully reaching the landing platform despite the weight of his grenades and ammunition, Burn crossed much of the port area to the two artillery turrets he had to destroy, near the inner caisson of the Joubert lock. On the way back, he was captured by three German soldiers that he inadvertently led to the British positions.

Blinded by the powerful searchlights, the two motorboats following ML *1* had both passed the Old Entrance. Commanded by naval Lieutenant Edward Burt, ML *2* carried Lieutenant John Morgan's protection squad and Lieutenant Mark Woodcock's assault group, whose mission it was to destroy the Old Entrance's swing bridge and the two neighboring

The Old Mole, seen from the other side. (J-C Stasi)

More than 70 years later, the Old Mole still bears the scars of March 28, 1942.
(Hubert Chemereau)

A British motorboat smolders near the port. (Bundesarchiv)

lock gates. After turning about, ML *2* managed to reach the Old Mole, but was immediately targeted by the guns of a harbor defense vessel. In the face of intense enemy fire, Woodcock and Morgan reembarked immediately and asked to be left on the other side of the Old Mole.

As they were pulling away, Lieutenant Smalley and his team, who had just blown up the operating station (or "winding shed") which controlled the mechanism that opened and closed the Joubert lock's outer caisson, arrived. They ran toward ML *2*, which Burt pulled in to berth once again, and managed to board. But Burt's decision to wait for them had catastrophic consequences: German shelling killed several people, including Smalley, and left several wounded; but worse was to come. When Burt and his crew had just made it past the end of the Old Mole and reached open sea, ML *2* was once again targeted by enemy artillery. Half a dozen men were killed and several others wounded, including Lieutenant Woodcock. ML *2* itself was done for, its burning remains drifting in the middle of the estuary for a good hour before finally sinking.

ML *3*, carrying several members of Lieutenant-Colonel Newman's staff, was equally unlucky. German artillery fire forced the commandos who had just disembarked to immediately scramble back on board. As it was pulling away, the motorboat was struck by several shells that instantly killed the commander, Lieutenant Eric Beart. The sailors and commandos had to abandon ship, throwing themselves into the water or into the rubber life rafts to escape the flames that now engulfed the boat. Among them was Warrant Office Alan Moss, who carried the flares that, once fired, would be the signal for all troops to withdraw.

But Moss never reached the shore, nor did his precious ammunition: he died rescuing another soldier from drowning. Of the 11 commandos on Beart's boat, only three survived.

ML *4* came to an even more violent end. Hit by several shells, it caught fire and exploded soon after, killing 15 of the 17 commandos and most of the sailors on board.

Micky Wynn's motorboat, MTB 74, successfully launched two time-delayed torpedoes at the gates of the Old Entrance. (Imperial War Museum)

The memorial to the British Commandos of World War II, in the Scottish Highlands. (Agusto757)

In Profile:
Sergeant Thomas Durrant VC

Thomas "Tommy" Frank Durrant VC (service no. 1874047) was born on October 17, 1918, in Green Street Green, Farnborough, Kent, UK, working as a butcher's boy and a builder's laborer after he left school. In early 1937, he enlisted in the Corps of Royal Engineers before volunteering for the Special Service Independent Companies that saw service in the Norway campaigns, where he received a field promotion to sergeant. On return from Norway, his unit was reformed as No. I Commando, with whom he saw action during Operation *Chariot*. His epic action against the Kriegsmarine torpedo boat, the *Jaguar*, earned him a posthumous Victoria Cross—Durrant had died of his wounds shortly after capture—at the behest of the German commander, Lieutenant-Commander F. K. Paul, who brought Durrant's valour to Lieutenant-Colonel Charles Newman's attention while the latter was a PoW. Durrant's citation reads in part:

> For great gallantry, skill and devotion to duty when in charge of a Lewis gun in HM Motor Launch 306 in the St Nazaire raid on 28 March 1942.
>
> Motor Launch 306 came under heavy fire while proceeding up the River Loire towards the port. Sergeant Durrant, in his position abaft the bridge, where he had no cover or protection, engaged enemy gun positions and searchlights ashore. During this engagement he was severely wounded in the arm but refused to leave his gun. The Motor Launch subsequently went down the river and was attacked by a German destroyer at 50 to 60 yards range, and often closer. In this action Sergeant Durrant continued to fire at the destroyer's bridge with the greatest of coolness and with complete disregard of the enemy's fire. The Motor Launch was illuminated by the enemy searchlight, and Sergeant Durrant drew on himself the individual attention of the enemy guns, and was again wounded in many places. Despite these further wounds he stayed in his exposed position, still firing his gun, although after a time only able to support himself by holding on to the gun mounting.
>
> After a running fight, the Commander of the German destroyer called on the Motor Launch to surrender. Sergeant Durrant's answer was a further burst of fire at the destroyer's bridge. Although now very weak, he went on firing, using drums of ammunition as fast as they could be replaced. A renewed attack by the enemy vessel eventually silenced the fire of the Motor Launch, but Sergeant Durrant refused to give up until the destroyer came alongside, grappled the Motor Launch and took prisoner those who remained alive.

Durrant died from his wounds on March 28, 1942, aged 23; he is buried in La Baule-Escoublac War Cemetery, France in Plot I, Row D, Grave 11.

A British soldier drenched with fuel takes refuge on an inflatable life raft. (Bundesarchiv)

Commanded by Lieutenant Leslie Fenton, known in Britain and the United States as a movie actor, ML 5 carried Captain Richard "Dickie" Hooper's commando team, responsible for neutralizing two positions near the Old Mole. Early on in the battle, a shell hit the deck and seriously wounded both Fenton and Hooper. Without steering and with one of her engines gone, the boat was forced to withdraw without a single commando disembarking.

ML 6, commanded by naval Lieutenant Mark Rodier, was carrying Warrant Officer George Haines's assault team, tasked with destroying the guns on the shore of the estuary. Despite the ceaseless shrapnel, the blinding searchlights, the burning fuel, the smoke and the blazing ruins of its fellow boats, ML 6's entire commando contingent managed to make it off the boat and into the dock.

But ML 6 did not escape the estuary. After collecting some of the *Campbeltown*'s passengers, including Lieutenant-Commander Sam Beattie, the boat was targeted by the coastal batteries and Lieutenant Rodier was killed by a shell. ML 6 burned for three hours, its deck covered with the dead and wounded. Most of the men who threw themselves into the water to escape the fire drowned or were killed by fuel burning on the surface. The few survivors, including Sam Beattie, were picked up by a German patrol boat in the early hours of March 28. But Nigel Tibbits, the main architect of the *Campbeltown*'s metamorphosis, never saw Britain again.

An additional boat, which was not part of the two attack columns, proceeded to the Old Entrance. Commanded by Lieutenant Neville Nock, ML16 was armed with torpedoes, but carried neither assault troops nor demolition teams. Its mission was to attack the enemy and pick up commandos for the return journey. The vessel fired furiously at the artillery batteries and floodlights on the docks, before stopping to rescue the sailors and commandos

In front of the large Ost 6 staff bunker, built between the rue de l'Écluse and the swing bridge, German soldiers support one of their own, wounded in the fighting. At bottom right is a wounded British soldier. (Bundesarchiv.)

stuck in the oily waters. In doing so, the boat itself caught fire and was immediately targeted by German artillery. Much of the crew was killed or wounded during this barrage and in the subsequent explosions.

Due to engine trouble, MTB *74* was a little late reaching the Old Entrance. But when the *Campbeltown* perfectly impacted its target and ruptured the Joubert lock's outer caisson, Wynn was there to launch his time-delayed torpedoes at the Old Entrance lock. Bursting from their tubes affixed to the bow of MTB *74*, the two huge projectiles plunged into the water, hitting the metal gates with a thud before sinking to the bottom of the estuary. If everything went to plan, the torpedoes would explode in a little over two hours.

As his mission was now completed, Ryder ordered Wynn to collect part of the *Campbeltown*'s crew and set sail for England. Wynn complied, and MTB *74* was soon heading out to sea at a speed of 40 knots. But when Wynn stopped to rescue two men clinging to a life raft, the boat was caught in a deluge of fire: some German gunners, having noticed its sudden deceleration, picked MTB *74* out as a prime target. Wynn was thrown off the bridge by a shell explosion and lost consciousness. When he came to his boat was on fire, his face bloodied and his left eye was hanging squarely out of its socket. His crew and the commandos had already deserted the stricken craft. The only other man on board was Chief Motor Mechanic W. H. Lovegrove, who helped his young commander to get up and board the life raft, which was already overloaded, the men who could not fit inside clinging to its sides.

With his remaining eye, Wynn watched helplessly hour after hour as his companions, unable to hold on, let go of the raft and disappeared into the icy waters. When a German gunboat discovered the raft early in the afternoon of March 28, only three men were left: Micky Wynn, Lovegrove and mechanic Able Seaman William Alfred Savage.

Shortly after MTB *74* set sail from the Old Entrance, Robert Ryder discovered the horror of what was happening farther west on the estuary. Until this point, convinced of the complete success of the operation, the naval commander had never imagined that the German batteries could cause so much carnage. He was shocked to discover so many of his boats burning or exploding amidst the flaming waters, to hear the howls of pain from men burning alive on their rudderless boats, who were drowning, who were trapped by searing oil slicks. But how could it have been otherwise? As soon as the diversionary air raid was over, all the searchlights and enemy guns protecting the port area turned to the water, creating chaos for the fragile wooden boats that were overloaded with men, equipment and fuel.

Faced with this atrocious spectacle, Ryder's mind likely returned to the ominous comment made by a commando before the flotilla left Falmouth: "These boats will burn like matchboxes."

Wounded in his right leg, Lance-Sergeant Stanley Davis is being supported by Corporal Herbert Shipton. The two commandos have just been captured and are being escorted by Kriegsmarine troops. (Bundesarchiv)

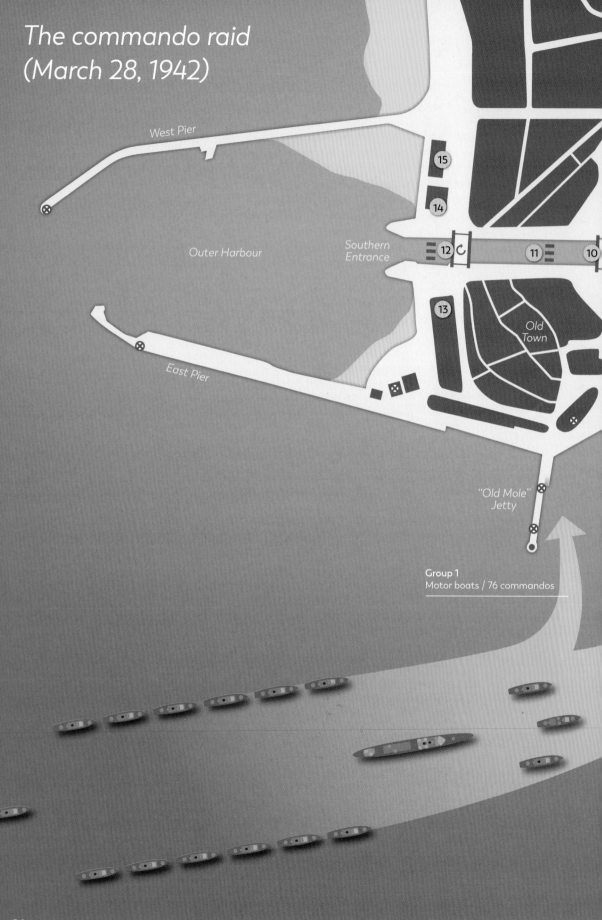

The commando raid
(March 28, 1942)

West Pier

15

14

Outer Harbour

Southern
Entrance

12

11

10

13

Old
Town

East Pier

"Old Mole"
Jetty

Group 1
Motor boats / 76 commandos

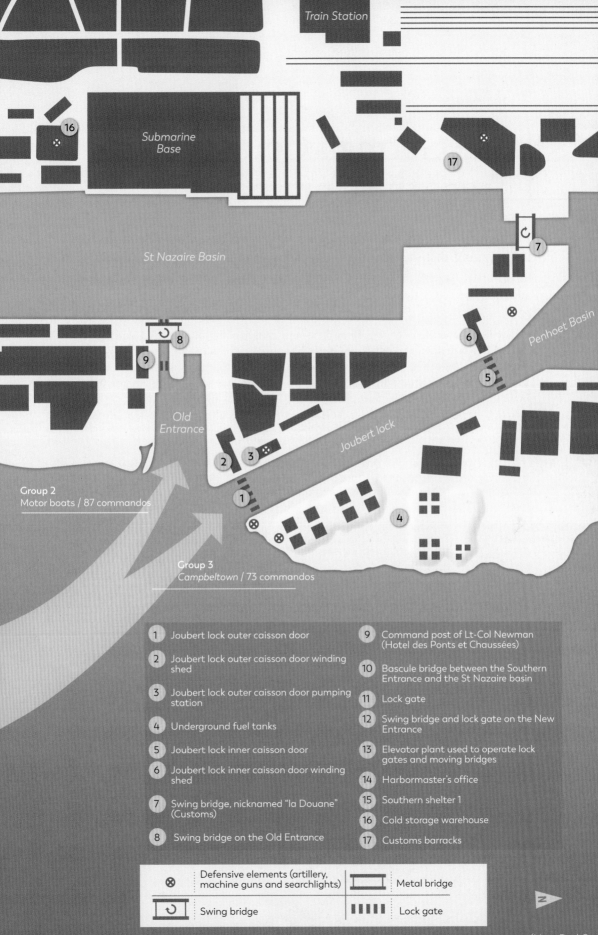

Train Station

Submarine
Base

16

17

St Nazaire Basin

7

6

5

Penhoet Basin

8

9

Old
Entrance

2 3

Joubert lock

1

4

Group 2
Motor boats / 87 commandos

Group 3
Campbeltown / 73 commandos

1	Joubert lock outer caisson door	9	Command post of Lt-Col Newman (Hotel des Ponts et Chaussées)
2	Joubert lock outer caisson door winding shed	10	Bascule bridge between the Southern Entrance and the St Nazaire basin
3	Joubert lock outer caisson door pumping station	11	Lock gate
4	Underground fuel tanks	12	Swing bridge and lock gate on the New Entrance
5	Joubert lock inner caisson door	13	Elevator plant used to operate lock gates and moving bridges
6	Joubert lock inner caisson door winding shed	14	Harbormaster's office
7	Swing bridge, nicknamed "la Douane" (Customs)	15	Southern shelter 1
8	Swing bridge on the Old Entrance	16	Cold storage warehouse
		17	Customs barracks

⊗ Defensive elements (artillery, machine guns and searchlights)

↻ Swing bridge

▭ Metal bridge

▮▮▮ Lock gate

N

(Map : Paul Gros)

The German Counterattack Traps the Commandos

As the hours passed, the Germans engaged more and more men against the invading British, tracking them through the port and the old town until early morning. Meanwhile, at sea, Kriegsmarine torpedo boats attacked the retreating forces.

A few minutes after *Campbeltown* rammed the outer caisson of the Joubert lock, Lieutenant-Colonel Newman disembarked. Accompanied by a small staff contingent, headed up by his faithful second-in-command Stan Day, "Colonel Charles," as Newman's men affectionately called him, strode down the wooden pier on the southern side of the Old Entrance. The group immediately headed to the building selected to serve as the command post for the operation, namely the Hotel des Ponts et Chaussées (Hotel of Bridges and Footpaths) located near the Old Entrance lock.

The first British prisoners are gathered outside bunker Ost 6, located near the swing bridge. From left: Lieutenant Gerrard Brett, Lieutenant Bill "Tiger" Watson, Private Tom McCormack and Lieutenant Stuart Chant (partially masked). The man on the stretcher is unidentified. Their state attests to the intensity of the fighting. (Bundesarchiv)

A photograph of St Nazaire old town, taken before the war. On the far left is the chimney of the elevator plant and in the foreground is the Old Mole jetty. It was through these narrow streets that the Germans hunted down the last of the British commandos on March 28, 1942. (Hubert Chemereau)

But before they could establish a base at the hotel, the men first had to clear the building of the Germans already there. This was complicated by artillery fire coming from the roof of the submarine base, just opposite, as well as the guns and machine guns of a minesweeper moored in the basin. Fortunately, Warrant Officer Haines's assault group was able to silence them with the help of a 2-inch mortar and a machine gun.

Meanwhile, a few hundred meters away, some commandos who had managed to disembark at the Old Mole jetty made for the New Entrance, including Captain William "Bill" Pritchard, accompanied by Lieutenant Philip Walton's demolition team, in charge of destroying the bridge closest to the St Nazaire basin—"Bridge D"—and Lieutenant Bill Watson's protection squad.

With the help of Corporal Ian Maclagan, Pritchard began by blowing up two tugboats moored together in the same berth, using charges placed between the two boats below the water level. After the blast, as Walton's demolition team had not yet arrived, Pritchard ordered the other three members of his squad to deal with the bascule bridge. Then, still accompanied by Maclagan, he moved on in search of new targets.

But for Captain Pritchard, Dunkirk veteran and now Group 1 and 2 demolitions officer, his raid was about to come to an abrupt halt. Just as he and Maclagan entered the old town on their way to the bridge that Walton was supposed to destroy, he got into a knife fight with a German and was killed.

As for Lieutenant Watson, who was leading his men through the old town, he was targeted by several machine guns firing from the roof of a house and on the other side of the basin. Having lost his bag of grenades, he waited until a lull in the firing to join his group, who had taken shelter behind a railcar. There, he also found Walton's demolition team.

Royal Navy raiding force

Operational Designation	Vessel Name	Commanding Officer	Comments
-	MGB 314	Lt Dunstan Curtis	Flotilla leader, destroyed
-	HMS Campbeltown	Lt-Cdr Stephen Beattie	Ram vessel, destroyed
ML 1	ML 192	Lt-Cdr W L Stephens	Destroyed
ML 2	ML 262	Lt Edward Burt	Destroyed
ML 3	ML 267	Lt Eric Beart	Destroyed
ML 4	ML 268	Lt Arnold Tillie	Destroyed
ML 5	ML 156	Lt Leslie Fenton	Scuttled
ML 6	ML 177	Lt Mark Rodier	Destroyed
ML 7	ML 270	Lt Stuart Irwin	Scuttled
ML 8	ML 160	Lt Thomas Boyd	Returned
ML 9	ML 447	Lt Thomas Platt	Destroyed
ML 10	ML 341	Lt Douglas Briault	Engine failure en route, returned
ML 11	ML 457	Lt Thomas Collier	Destroyed
ML 12	ML 307	Lt Norman Wallis	Returned
ML 13	ML 443	Lt Kenneth Horlock	Returned
ML 14	ML 306	Lt Ian Henderson	Salvaged by Germans
ML 15	ML 446	Lt Henry Falconer	Scuttled
ML 16	ML 298	Lt Neville Robert Nock	Destroyed
17	MTB 74	S/Lt Michael Wynn	Destroyed

Surprised to see them without their commander, he asked for news of the man he loved like a brother. Just as Lance-Sergeant Richard Bradley was about to answer the lieutenant, the sergeant was mowed down by a burst of machine-gun fire.

After repeatedly escaping enemy fire, "Tiger" Watson finally managed to reach Newman's command post, weaving his way through a maze of hangars and warehouses. Shortly after his arrival, the fear that had been growing in his stomach was confirmed: his dear friend Philip Walton was dead.

***

To say that Herbert Sohler was confused when he was informed of the raid would be something of an understatement. In the middle of the night at his La Baule villa, the lieutenant-commander received a telephone call and, on hearing the news of the British raid, snapped: "An English landing in St Nazaire? You must be drunk, please hang up!"

But when the harbormaster confirmed that half of the port facilities were in enemy hands, the 7th U-boat Flotilla commander made haste to the officers' mess. Welcomed by bursts of laughter and mocking remarks, Sohler had to raise his voice to convince his staff to seek shelter, away from St Nazaire, until the all-clear. Due to their extensive training, German submariners were expressly forbidden from engaging in infantry combat.

After telephoning Admiral Dönitz to inform him of the situation, Sohler called his driver and immediately headed in the direction of St Nazaire, 10 kilometers away. En route, he was impressed by the extent of the artillery barrage; the night was shaken by intermittent explosions from the estuary and harbor.

When he arrived at St Nazaire, the lieutenant-commander was relieved to find the base still in German hands. A quick tour of the facilities reassured him that all was still well; on his orders, explosive charges were placed in all immobilized submarines. In addition, dredgers stationed in the basin were moved to protective positions in front of the berths.

While Sohler called Dönitz to reassure him of the safety of his prized U-boats, the defensive capability in the port continued to grow. Following the disembarkation alert sounded by Captain Mecke at 0130, the first elements of the 703rd and 705th Naval Artillery Battalions arrived via the bridges at the Southern Entrance. They were joined by the mixed-sex combat groups formed from the base's security personnel. Moving north by way of the swing bridge separating the St Nazaire and Penhoët basins, they met strong resistance from the commandos of Lieutenant Roderick's team.

The German counterattack continued to grow in size and intensity. Placed on alert at about 0140, the men of the 679th Infantry Regiment left their barracks between Guérande and Pontchâteau, about 30 kilometers from St Nazaire. Well-equipped and well-trained, with 12 machine guns per company, the men of this unit were professional soldiers, unlike the logistics and administrative personnel who were filling in and whose firearm experience amounted to little more than a few shooting exercises.

As soon as they arrived in theater, the Germans encountered the British, who, respective missions accomplished, were heading for Newman's command post, a rallying point for the reembarkation from the Old Mole. To get there, the commandos had no alternative but to cross the bridge at the Old Entrance—"Bridge G"—which was being valiantly held by Captain Roy's Scots.

Seeing that the bridge was right in the firing line of a machine gun positioned on the roof of a neighboring building, Stuart Chant ordered his men to cross it by clinging to its

A German patrol in old St Nazaire. Most of these troops belonged to the Kriegsmarine. The man in the center is carrying an MP40 machine pistol. (Bundesarchiv)

91

steel beams. When his own turn came, Chant was forced to hang on painfully by his wrists due to the injuries on his hands sustained on board the *Campbeltown*.

Chant and his four sergeants found Newman and his staff behind a shed near the quay where Warrant Officer Haines had set up his mortar a few minutes earlier. "Colonel Charles" had left his command post to be closer to his men. Chant was as impressed by Newman's gaiety and bonhomie as were Burn, Purdon, and the other team leaders, the lieutenant-colonel staying true to form despite the situation. From his somewhat landlocked position, Newman probably had little real knowledge of the drama being played out in the estuary, and after having seen and heard the explosions emanating from the Joubert lock sector, the successive reports coming in from the team leaders bolstered his optimism. His jocular manner with his assistants Bill Copland and Stan Day comforted the men arriving at the quay, one after the other, though most of them were wounded and all of them sweaty and covered with dust and soot.

After listening to the reports, Newman decided that it was time to withdraw. All that remained now was to launch the flares to notify Captain Roy and Lieutenant Roderick, a few hundred meters farther north, to pull back. But as Sergeant-Major Moss had been

Captured at the harbor alongside Private Paddy Bushe, Captain Michael Burn flashes the "V for victory" sign as he finds himself the subject of a German propaganda photographer. (Bundesarchiv)

In 2009, back in St Nazaire for an anniversary of the raid, Michael Burn recreates his pose, 67 years later. (Press-Ocean-Franck Labarre Archives)

killed, and his precious cargo of flares lost, Newman ordered Lance-Corporal Harrington to verbally alert the officers of the two groups that it was time to fall back. After the exchange of passwords with the commandos posted at the Old Entrance Bridge—"War weapons week"–"Weymouth"—Harrington turned right toward the northern end of the Joubert lock. Along the way, he met Roderick, already pulling back. With his message transmitted, Harrington left Roderick immediately to report to Newman. Harrington would later be rewarded for his bravery and efficiency during those crucial minutes with the Military Medal.

With the deaths of Pritchard and Walton, and the disaster that had befallen Smalley's team, not to mention all the men unable to land in the first place or those who had been killed in action, there were only 70 commandos left to regroup on Newman.

Accompanied by Bill Copland, "Colonel Charles" began advancing to the Old Mole jetty. As the two officers emerged from the hangar area, they came to an immediate stop, horrified by the spectacle before them. Due to the oil slicks from the wrecked motorboats, it appeared as if the entire estuary was on fire. Near the jetty itself, some burnt-out hulls smoldered. Searchlights and gunfire intermittently lit up the sky, which was streaked with billowing flames. Not a single encouraging noise came from this inferno. The only sounds were the crackling of the fires and, from time to time, the heart-rending cries of a man being incinerated.

Newman, joined by the commandos massing behind him, knew that escaping by sea was now impossible. All the ships had been blown up or had left so there was no means of transport. Keeping up appearances Newman remarked "This is where we walk home."

At dawn on March 28, German soldiers carry a dead British commando from his hiding place. (Bundesarchiv)

Returning to the hangar area, Newman took shelter behind a wagon with Bill Copland and Stan Day for an informal briefing. The situation was critical but clear: straight ahead, the Old Mole was still firmly held by the enemy; on both sides was the flaming water that had already claimed so many British lives; behind was the harbor, where more and more Germans were breaking through at the New Entrance, across the bridges that were still intact.

When Newman suggested that under the circumstances it would not be dishonorable for them to surrender, Copland's response cut to the quick: "Certainly not, colonel! All we need to do is open up a path."

Emboldened by his right-hand man, Newman decided to try and escape the town. To do so, they first had to establish a secure perimeter to protect themselves from the enemy advance. The Germans were progressing so quickly now that it was becoming difficult in such poor visibility to distinguish friend from foe. Fortunately for the British, they had their blue torches and white straps on their uniforms, and the Germans wore boots that were heavy and noisy.

With so few troops, half of whom were wounded, Newman asked Copland to divide the force into small groups, each under the command of an officer. The quickest way out of the harbor would be to cross the Old Town Square and attempt to cross at "Bridge D," which Lieutenant Walton's team had blown up. But with the Germans beginning to take control, Newman decided to bypass the hangar area where the enemy could attack at will from any direction.

It was about 0300, an hour and a half after the landing, when the surviving commandos left their positions, the assault troops and protection teams in front and the demolition crews, less well-armed, following behind. The ranks began thinning as they progressed, targeted by snipers and grenades, the wounded collapsing, incapable of continuing.

Arriving at the quay, the British were then targeted by the batteries located on the opposite side of the St Nazaire basin, and by infantry firing from the hangars just behind them. Several men were shot, including "Tiger" Watson, who asked his friends to leave him behind after being given a shot of morphine.

From here, the commandos had to turn left and move along the quay to the Old Town Square, cross the square—fortunately across its shortest side—and finally reach "Bridge D," the last hope of escape. But the bridge was still 50 meters away across open ground, subjected to the fire of the machine guns posted on the roofs and at the windows of the houses, as well as rifle fire from infantry positioned along the quay on other side of the bridge.

As soon as Warrant Officer Haines had set up his machine gun in support, "Colonel Charles" turned to his men and shouted for all he was worth: "Forward, lads!" The commandos lurched forward as one, encouraged by Donald Roy, who continued shouting: "Move! Move!"

German sailors display the Kriegsmarine flag flown by the *Campbeltown* until its arrival at the Loire estuary, a flag that bears the markings of its London-based manufacturer. (Bundesarchiv)

A Kriegsmarine helmet, discovered in the grounds of Pignerolle Castle, near Angers, where Admiral Dönitz had transferred his command post and the communications center for all submarines based in France, following the British raid on St Nazaire, in a move away from the coast. (Private collection)

A German MP40 machine pistol, or "Schmeisser," in reference to its designer, Hugo Schmeisser. This weapon was used throughout the German armed forces from 1940, an effective weapon of 9mm caliber, with a 32-cartridge magazine, a practical range of 100 meters, and a firing rate of 500–600 rounds per minute. (Private collection)

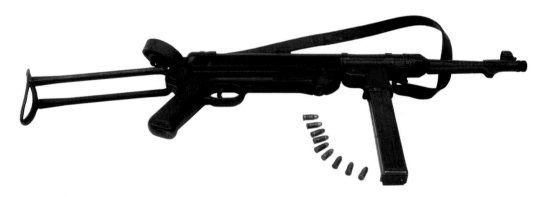

As they gradually approached the bridge, passing Lieutenant Walton's body, the commandos suffered additional losses, but were relieved to see the Germans on the other side of the lock get up and fall back.

Leaving more and more dead and wounded behind them, Newman's men finally reached the bridge, which they could feel vibrating through their rubber-soled boots. Bullets whistled over their heads, ricocheting loudly off the steel girders before vanishing into the darkness. Yet more men were hit as they poured across the bridge. Injured by grenade shrapnel in his leg and shoulder, Lieutenant Corran Purdon raced forward until he ran into the massive Stan Day.

Following the example of Major Copland, who was heading directly for a particularly deadly machine-gun position, the commandos who managed to get across attacked any Germans standing in their way with sub-machine guns, grenades, and even knives.

The British were now on the other side of the bridge, with the strongly defended submarine base on their right and the new town ahead of them. Beyond that was the countryside, and the possibility of escape. When a Kübelwagen bristling with German machine-gunners suddenly appeared at an intersection, the surviving commandos all opened up at the same time, and the vehicle careened into a café window, killing all the vehicle occupants.

Next, a German armored personnel carrier appeared, hurtling towards them at full speed, swerving wildly until it finally came to a stop a hundred meters away at an intersection, blocking the road directly ahead of the commandos. As it was now impossible to proceed directly, what remained of the British force veered left and split off into small groups, each trying their luck down a different street.

Minute by minute, the German presence was becoming stronger. Infantry now patrolled every street and alley, with machine guns, and armored vehicles positioned at every intersection.

In a last-ditch attempt to escape, the British survivors began to abandon the streets and alleyways to undertake what they would later call "the St Nazaire steeplechase," climbing walls, sprinting through courtyards and gardens, and hurdling chicken coops.

Sergeant Stewart Deery (No. 12 Commando) and Corporal Frederick Holt (No. 2 Commando) greet their captors with smiles. (Bundesarchiv)

But exhausted and short of ammunition, and with their wounded on the verge of collapse, the commandos eventually had to stop running and seek refuge. While looking for water for his wounded comrades, Donald Roy entered a house where he was immediately captured by the Germans who had established a guard post there.

With dawn approaching, Newman decided to take the 20 or so commandos accompanying him down into the basement of a house that had been converted into an air-raid shelter. His original plan was to hide out in the basement all day, then send his men up in twos and threes to escape under the cover of darkness. But as time passed, his mind began to turn toward the possibility of surrender. He knew that the Germans would eventually find them and that, in their weakened state and with so many wounded, any attempt at resistance would be suicidal.

Meanwhile, the wounded were laid out on benches and on the floor, while their comrades tried to relieve some of their pain. At the top of the stairs, Sergeant David Steele stood guard. The minutes passed, surprisingly quiet after the hell of the previous few hours. Some of the men lit up cigarettes, the first in a long time.

Suddenly, the sound of boots filled the air. Germans had just entered the house and gone upstairs, executing their orders to search every building in town. The commandos who were still able straightened up and grabbed their weapons, almost by reflex.

After their capture, British commandos and sailors were gathered in a local restaurant before being transferred to a PoW camp. Despite their situation, they seem far from beaten. (Bundesarchiv)

The crew of ML *1*, destroyed before reaching the Old Entrance, are all smiles despite having become prisoners of war. (Bundesarchiv)

After a few tense moments, the footsteps faded. The commandos breathed a sigh of relief—but it was premature. Realizing that it was all over, Newman rushed up the stairs to surrender before shots were fired.

Bill Copland, reflecting 30 years after the fact, recalled the absurdity of the situation. Copland thought the Germans had arrived in a ridiculous way. If they had thrown a couple of grenades from the top of the stairs, the commandos would have died. But they did not. If the roles were reserved, they would never have taken so many risks. Copland believed the Germans were inexperienced soldiers in comparison to the commandos, who knew exactly what to do and that it was over for them.

The commandos were unceremoniously disarmed and forced up to the ground floor. Hands in the air, they were marched across the street and, to their great surprise, brought into the house directly opposite the one they'd been hiding in. Newman couldn't help but smile at the thought that the place he'd chosen as a refuge for his men was just a few meters away from the enemy HQ.

***

While the surviving commandos were being systematically rounded up in St Nazaire, the rescue motorboats were attempting to escape the powerful coastal batteries along the banks of the estuary. Their objective was point "Y," about 60 kilometers west of St Nazaire, where they would meet up with their "guard dogs," the *Atherstone* and the *Tynedale*.

In the early hours of March 28, 1942, being too far off to see what was happening in the estuary, the commanders of the two destroyers, Lieutenant-Commander "Jumbo" Jenks and

Sergeant Durrant (No. 1 Commando) fought to the point of exhaustion— his ammunition virtually depleted—on ML *14* against the *Jaguar*. He was posthumously awarded the Victoria Cross. (Imperial War Museum)

Lieutenant-Commander Hugh Tweedie respectively, were starting to worry. By this point, most of the flotilla should have been en route to the rendezvous, but only five motorboats had issued the "withdrawing" signal, and those between 0218 and 0325. Moreover, the two commanders were aware of the five German torpedo boats that had sailed the previous evening from St Nazaire.

Of the 17 motorboats engaged in the final phase of Operation *Chariot*, seven had been destroyed near the Old Mole jetty or the Old Entrance; and two others were terminally damaged shortly after leaving the harbor: Micky Wynn's MTB *74* and Lieutenant Rodier's ML *6*.

As dawn approached, a new drama visited what was left of the flotilla, and specifically Lieutenant Ian Henderson's ML *14*, which left St Nazaire after failing to land Lieutenant John Vanderwerve's protection squad and Lieutenant Ronald Swayne's demolition team.

Well ahead of schedule, ML *14* was speeding toward the rendezvous. Shortly before 0530, Henderson discerned through the mist, on the port side, large white streaks that he could not identify. After a few minutes, the mist cleared enough for him to use his powerful marine binoculars to discern three vessels of the 5th Torpedo-boat Flotilla.

Immediately, Henderson stopped his engines and asked Lieutenants Swayne and Vanderwerve to get their commandos to battle stations in the utmost silence. Henderson was no fool—he knew full well that his little wooden boat had no chance against these 800-ton steel monsters, twice as fast as his and with nearly a dozen guns apiece, including three 105mm guns—but he was not about to go down without a fight.

The first torpedo boat passed to port, and then the second; but the third, the *Jaguar*, commanded by Lieutenant-Commander Friedrich Paul, came out of file and swept the last of the darkness with a searchlight until the beam illuminated the British motorboat.

The two ships opened fire at almost the same time, the first British salvo shattering the *Jaguar*'s searchlight. Another searchlight immediately lit up. Preferring to capture the boat than sink it, as he would later assert, the German commander decided not to use his 105mm guns that would have dealt his adversary a fatal blow. Instead he used his heavy machine guns, killing and injuring several men, and inflicting heavy damage on the hull and superstructure of the ML *14*.

The *Jaguar* began to approach the still-illuminated motorboat, still firing. Realizing that the Germans were going to try to board, Henderson ordered his men to destroy the enemy port-side rudder. The torpedo boat, however, rammed the ML *14* amidships, hard enough to throw several men into the sea. Lieutenant Vanderwerve disappeared beneath the waves. As for Ordinary Seaman Rees, sucked under by the wash of the propellers, his toes were severed but fortunately he was rescued.

The two boats were now so close that the British and Germans were shooting at almost point-blank range, with increasing intensity. Shouts and screams rent the air.

After pulling back a fraction, the *Jaguar* then opened fire with its 20mm guns, claiming yet more victims. One of the guns destroyed the last Oerlikon still in working order at the stern of the motorboat.

The crew of the crippled ML *14* were transferred to a smaller boat after being picked up by the *Jaguar* torpedo boat. At the time this photograph was taken, they were waiting to land on the quay at St Nazaire. (Bundesarchiv)

The survivors of the ML *14* have just arrived at St Nazaire. Wounded, Corporal Salisbury (No. 1 Commando) is being supported by Seaman Batteson and Lieutenant Ronnie Swayne. On the left, in the background, is Sub-Lieutenant Philip Dark, second-in-command aboard the ML *14*. (St Nazaire Ecomuseum)

Despite the injuries he had sustained while attempting to berth at the Old Mole jetty, Sergeant Tom Durrant managed to grab a Bren light machine gun and opened fire until the last cartridge was spent.

A new salvo from the torpedo boat destroyed the bridge, mortally wounding Lieutenant Henderson and throwing his second-in-command, Sub-Lieutenant Philip Dark, into a corner where he lay crumpled and unconscious.

Coming up from the hold where he had been searching for ammunition, Swayne stumbled upon a scene of desolation: the bridge, awash with blood, was littered with dead and wounded, limbs entangled. Looking up, the commando officer then saw in the pale light of dawn the *Jaguar* approaching again, ready to administer the coup de grâce now that its prey was done for.

Cutting through the silence that followed the clamor of the preceding moments, a warning—in English—reached the handful of survivors of ML *14*: "Cease fire! Do not shoot anymore!"

The effect of this invitation to surrender was as swift as it was brutal: a sudden burst of heavy fire from the motorboat directed at the *Jaguar*. In spite of his multiple wounds, Durrant had made his way to the Lewis double machine guns and opened fire on the torpedo boat with the kind of energy that comes only from desperation, and was soon joined in his efforts by Corporal E. Evans.

Lieutenant-Commander Paul repeated his warning, bringing his boat to within meters of the crippled wooden boat. As Durrant, half-slumped over his gun, responded once again with a long burst of fire, the *Jaguar* pulled back until, having opened up enough distance, it again opened fire.

On board the motorboat, gunner Ralph Batteson ventured onto the sticky, cluttered bridge, picking his way through debris and body parts to reach Sergeant Durrant, whose bloodied body was riddled with bullets.

"Come on, old man," he said, trying to support him.

"I'm done for, help the others," Durrant murmured, fading fast.

"I'm afraid we can't keep going," Swayne admitted, regretfully, before turning to inform his German counterpart that this time, they really were done fighting.

It was approximately 0630. This fight to the death between unmatched opponents had lasted about an hour. Of the 28 men aboard the motorboat, only eight were still standing; all the others were dead or wounded.

Once aboard the German torpedo boat, the survivors of ML *14* were treated with kindness. The wounded were taken to the wardroom and the officers' cabins by order of the commander. The latter, who spoke good English, even invited Swayne to have a drink with him, congratulating the commando officer, and his comrades, for their bravery.

Carried aboard the *Jaguar* in critical condition, Durrant and Henderson died a few minutes later, as the torpedo ship began to make its way back to St Nazaire. As for Sub-

The survivors of ML *14* gather on the pier after their violent clash with the *Jaguar*. (Bundesarchiv)

Wounded British commandos being evacuated during Operation *Archery*, the Maloy Raid, Vaagso island, Norway, December 27, 1941. (National Museum of the US Navy 11609-4 (LC-USZ62-89343)

Able Seaman William Savage VC

Able Seaman William Alfred Savage VC was born on October 30, 1912 in Smethwick, Staffordshire, England; he later moved to Winston Green, Birmingham after getting married. The citation for his posthumous award of the Victoria Cross for his part in Operation *Chariot*, written by Commander R. E. D. Ryder, reads in part:

> Able Seaman Savage showed conspicuous [gallantry and] skill and devotion to duty as gun layer of the pom pom in M.G. 314 during the St. Nazaire Raid. Completely exposed and under heavy fire from time to time, he engaged positions ashore with great accuracy. He also replied with vigorous and accurate fire against ships which attacked us on the way out. It is regretted that Savage was killed at his gun, but he is submitted that his high standard of devotion to duty should be recognised.

A postscript, written by the Coastal Forces Veterans, mentions:

> [Savage's] widow Doris, reluctantly had to sell his Victoria Cross (VC) and other medals in 1990, and the former Coastal Forces Veterans Association were instrumental in helping to raise part of the £55,000 needed to purchase them for the National Maritime Museum at Greenwich, where they are now kept. More recently, on learning that the VC had been locked away in the museum for the past eight years due to lack of available display space, and only available for viewing by appointment, Sandwell Council which covers Smethwick, made a loan request to the Maritime Museum for the medal to be displayed in his home town.

Lieutenant Dark, his scant medical knowledge kept him particularly busy during his forced return to port; as there was no doctor aboard the *Jaguar*, it was he who tended the wounded British and Germans.

As his prisoners disembarked at St Nazaire, Lieutenant-Commander Paul ordered his crew to attention in tribute to such valiant opponents.

***

As ML *14*'s struggle was drawing to a close, another sea battle was just beginning. As the *Atherstone* and *Tynedale* waited for the motorboats to join them, the latter, patrolling about 8 kilometers southwest of the motorboat route, spotted the other four German torpedo boats of the 5th Torpedo-boat Flotilla.

The engagement lasted less than 10 minutes, punctuated by a few strikes on each side, without any of the craft being sunk. Eventually, the Germans dispersed when the *Tynedale* took cover behind a smokescreen.

As day broke, the two escort destroyers were finally able to rendezvous with the surviving motorboats. Targeted by all the coastal batteries from the moment it left the harbor, MGB *314* was riddled with holes. It was, however, still going strong, thanks in large part to the skill of its commander, Dunstan Curtis, who was able to plane at full speed to avoid the incoming shells.

There were so many casualties among the crew of the *Campbeltown* that the boat "looked like an abattoir," according to Ryder, though he and the other officers on board were miraculously uninjured. Unfortunately, the gunner Bill Savage, so effective with his Vickers "pom-pom" gun, was finally killed, along with his comrade Able Seaman Frank Smith.

***

The blue sky and the calm sea offered perfect visibility when, just before 0800, MGB *314*, ML *5*, ML *15* and ML *7* joined the two destroyers. ML *7* was in such bad shape that it had to be abandoned after its crew and its commandos were transferred onto the *Atherstone*. The wounded from the other boats were divided between the two destroyers, where the doctors and nurses on board immediately set to work. There were so many men to be treated and amputations to be carried out that the officers' mess had to be turned into an operating theater, as there wasn't enough room in the infirmary.

Faced with so many casualties, so many terrified faces, and so much blood washing over the floors, the crews of the two destroyers were convinced that Operation *Chariot* had failed. When asked by the *Atherstone*'s commander if this was the case, following a pessimistic report from one of the motorboat commanders, a surviving commando proudly responded, "No, sir, it was a success!"

Robert Jenks received a similar answer from Ryder, sitting on the bridge where they had just been served coffee: "I don't see why you would call it a failure," Ryder stated calmly, noting that the *Campbeltown* had successfully rammed into the outer caisson, the explosive charges on board set, that he had nearly been killed by debris from the destruction of the pumping station, and that he had seen Micky Wynn successfully fire, on his command, two torpedoes at the Old Entrance lock.

Able Seaman William Alfred Savage was posthumously awarded the Victoria Cross for his heroic actions during the engagement between MGB *314* and the minesweeper *Sperrbrecher 137*. (Imperial War Museum)

As the small convoy started out on its journey homeward, a Heinkel 111 appeared above, swooping low over the vessels. However, the German airmen seemed content with sinking the already abandoned ML *7* before it disappeared, without picking a fight.

A few moments later, the British were overjoyed to spot an RAF Beaufighter overhead, though their spirits were soon lowered when they saw it was being followed by a Junkers 88. Hypnotized, the sailors and commandos watched the RAF pilot attack the German bomber so relentlessly that the two aircraft collided and crashed into the sea.

A little later that morning, the *Cleveland* and *Brocklesby*, the two additional destroyers promised by Admiral Forbes, appeared. The commander of the *Cleveland*, Commander Guy Sayer, took command of the entire flotilla, giving Ryder and his team a chance to rest.

As the hours passed, aircraft activity over the British naval force became more and more intense. The 19th Coastal Command Group made a total of 20 sorties throughout the return trip, losing two aircraft but shooting down four.

Slowed down by the damaged motorboats, the convoy was making unsatisfactory progress. The condition of some of the wounded was becoming more and more serious and it was becoming critical that they were taken to hospital as soon as possible. In the early afternoon, Sayer decided to scuttle MGB *314*, ML *7* and ML *15* in order to reach an English port as quickly as possible.

***

The *Tynedale* and *Atherstone* reached Plymouth that evening. The wounded were immediately taken ashore and transferred to the nearest hospitals. But the escort mission was not over yet: ML *8*, ML *12* and ML *13* were still somewhere at sea. Since they had been unable to make contact with the destroyers at point "Y," they had continued on a westerly heading, before turning north. The *Cleveland* and *Brocklesby* were tasked with searching for them with the help of three additional destroyers.

Two RAF aircraft followed overhead as the reunited convoy made its way towards the Scilly Isles. After a fraught journey, during which they repelled several air attacks and shot down a Heinkel 111, the convoy arrived in Falmouth on March 29, early in the morning.

***

While some semblance of calm had returned to St Nazaire, Herbert Sohler was shocked by the sight that greeted him in the early morning of Saturday, March 28, 1942. The boats in the basin had been sunk; only their masts and funnels jutted out above the surface of the water. On the quays, there was nothing but smoldering ruins, burnt debris, overturned cranes, shell craters, twisted beams, and wherever he looked dead enemy troops, the German corpses having already been removed.

Sohler was particularly intrigued by the old destroyer embedded in the outer caisson of the Joubert lock, its stern totally submerged in steel. He wondered why the British had sacrificed so much, so many of their men, for such a poor result. It would take several

On Sunday, March 28, 1942, early in the morning, German officers and technicians examine the *Campbeltown* embedded in the Joubert lock. In the background, on the left is the Old Mole jetty and one of the two bunkers, and on the right are the hangars and the Old Town, where fierce fighting had just taken place. (Bundesarchiv)

In Profile:
MTB *74* and the *Jaguar*

Motor Torpedo Boat *74*: This very fast motorboat, commanded by Lieutenant Micky Wynn, was originally tasked with firing two 700kg time-delayed torpedoes against the outer caisson of the Normandie Dock, in case the *Campbeltown* failed to hit its target. Since the destroyer succeeded, MTB 74 ended up firing its two torpedoes against the lock of the Old Entrance.

German Torpedo Boat *Jaguar* Type 1924. Fitted out on August 15, 1929, the *Jaguar* was part of the 5th Torpedo-boat Flotilla, which clashed with the British flotilla on its return home at dawn on March 28, 1942. It fought ML *14* for almost one hour, until the British forces, and ammunition, were exhausted.

Technical specifications

Built entirely of wood

Length: 21.3 meters (70 ft)

Width/beam: 5.5 meters (18 ft)

Displacement: 35 tons

Propulsion: 3 × engines, 12 × Packard gasoline
cylinders (1,200hp), 2 × Vosper V8 auxiliary engines

Max speed: 40 knots

Armament: 2 × 700kg 457mm torpedoes

Crew: 2 officers and 8 men

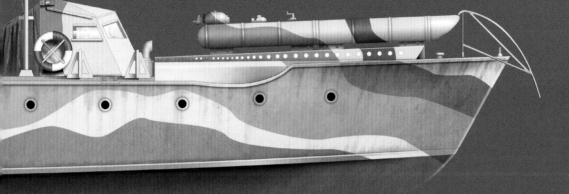

Technical specifications

Length: 92.6 meters (305 ft)

Width/beam: 8.6 meters (24 ft 6 in)

Displacement: 1,320 tons

Propulsion: 3 × steam boilers, 2 × Schichau-Werke
steam turbines

Power: 25,500hp

Maximum speed: 35.2 knots

Armament: 3 × 105mm Utofs guns, 2 × 20mm
antiaircraft guns, 6 × 500mm torpedo tubes,
30 × magnetic mines

Crew: 125 (Commander: Lt Friedrich Karl Paul)

(Thierry Vallet)

German Order of Battle

KRIEGSMARINE

809th German Marine Artillery Group

22nd Naval Flak Brigade

280th Naval Artillery Battalion

703rd Naval Artillery Battalion

705th Naval Artillery Battalion

5th Torpedo-boat Flotilla

6th U-boat Flotilla

7th U-boat Flotilla

16th Minesweeper Flotilla

42nd Minesweeper Flotilla

Torpedo boat *Jaguar*

armed trawler

Sperrbrecher 137

Naval Protection Force

Harbour Defence Companies

HEER

333rd Infantry Division

679th Infantry Regiment

tugboats to extricate it, he could not help thinking, as infantry picked through the bodies, collecting weapons and matériel.

The last of the British commandos were flushed out from their hiding places with Schmeissers and grenades. Discovered in the boiler room where he was hiding with Private Paddy Bushe, Captain Micky Burn posed for the camera as he was marched out with a rifle barrel in his back.

In his autobiography, *Turned Towards the Sun*, Burn commented "seeing that a German team were photographing us for Goebbels's propaganda, I formed my fingers into the V-sign."

For some, things had taken a more tragic turn. Wounded once again in the legs, Lieutenant Stuart Chant was found by an enemy patrol at approximately 0400, lying on the quay of the St Nazaire basin, unable to move, another commando at his side. His companion was killed, but Chant's life was spared because he was seriously wounded and because of his officer status.

As they surrendered or were captured, the able-bodied were gathered in a café to await transfer to a PoW camp. Despite the armed guards, the atmosphere in the cramped space was not oppressive.

Newman described it as being like a family reunion. Morale was good because the men all felt that they had done a very good job. As each man arrived, a little more detail could be added to their knowledge of the previous hours.

This good mood, which contrasted sharply with the reality of their situation, had another source. All the prisoners, able and wounded alike, knew that they had one more surprise up their sleeves: the explosives aboard the *Campbeltown* …

The Price of Success

The explosion of the *Campbeltown* late in the morning of March 28 made the Joubert lock unusable until the end of the war. The raid was thus a success—although not all the objectives were achieved—but at a cost of 169 dead and 232 prisoners for the British.

As the morning of Saturday, March 28, 1942 progressed, the unusual spectacle of a British destroyer embedded in the Joubert lock attracted more and more German spectators. After the senior officers whom the admiral commanding the port allowed to board first, military visitors flocked from all the units in the area; besides their own curiosity, they were attracted by the rumor that the still-smoking destroyer contained astronomical quantities of food and rare delicacies: chocolate, whisky, cigarettes, and real coffee …

Convinced that they had managed to defeat the British before the latter could complete their operation, the defenders of St Nazaire, as well as the sailors and submariners, were jubilant in the bright sunshine.

The *Campbeltown* explosion rendered the Joubert lock unusable until the end of the war. (St Nazaire Ecomuseum)

After receiving authorization from the admiral commanding the port, German troops took turns visiting the *Campbeltown* on the morning of March 28, 1942. (Bundesarchiv)

Meanwhile, a few hundred yards away, Lieutenant-Commander Sam Beattie, wrapped in a blanket since being pulled out of the icy estuary following the destruction of ML16 a few hours earlier, was being interrogated.

While the German officer questioning Beattie was courteous and spoke excellent English, he learnt little from the shaggy *Campbeltown* commander, who merely watched him, smoking a cigarette. Frustrated, the German officer became more forceful, informing Beattie that his raid was a failure and that the damaged caisson would be repaired in less than a month.

"It's absurd to think you could destroy a caisson like that with such a light boat," he added.

And that was all he said: an explosion of phenomenal violence shook the entire room, shaking the walls and shattering the windows. Under his blanket, the phlegmatic Beattie felt a shudder of excitement running through his body.

"That, I think, is proof that we did not underestimate the caisson," Beattie replied, as calmly as if he were still at the helm of his destroyer, sailing full steam ahead toward the Joubert lock.

It was approximately 1030 GMT (1130 local time).

Under the pressure of the explosion, the already bent caisson collapsed inward into the lock, with the massive shockwave ramming the two tankers in for repair up against the walls.

The explosion could be heard for miles around. Throughout the city, debris fell on houses, streets, courtyards, and gardens.

All those aboard the *Campbeltown* at the time were killed; not just German soldiers, but also workers from the Todt Organization employed on the submarine base. For several days after the explosion, locals found human remains and body parts on roofs, scattered on the ground, hanging from electric cables and telephone wires, stuck to walls or floating in the water, within a radius of about two kilometers from the site of the explosion. It was impossible to determine how many were killed, but estimates place the figure between 150 and 380 people.

In the room where the British were gathered, the explosion was greeted with applause and shouts of jubilation. Captured commandos and sailors laughed even as their guardians rushed to the doors in fear.

In the hours that followed, calm—or at least the illusion of calm—gradually returned to St Nazaire. Traffic flow was restored, with the obvious exception of the port area, which was closed off to all but a few authorized personnel.

That same day, the German high command broadcast an official statement on the raid over the international airwaves. In order to minimize the impact of the operation, there was no mention of the *Campbeltown* explosion:

> This Saturday, shortly after midnight, British planes flew over the region of St Nazaire in several waves, and dropped a number of bombs that caused no damage. While the Flak batteries were occupied with shooting at the planes, certain

Lieutenant-Commander Sam Beattie, commander of the *Campbeltown*, was being interrogated by German officers when the destroyer exploded. (Bundesarchiv)

PART OF THE GERMAN HIGH COMMAND COMMUNIQUE 1420/28/3.

(REUTER'S EDITION)

B3 B4

As has been announced by special communique, English naval forces attempted during the night of March 27th to land troops in the Loire Estuary in order to attack the submarine base at St. Nazaire and destroy the harbour gates.

Under fire of German naval batteries an old American destroyer laden with explosives, which was to have rammed the lock gates, blew up into the air before attaining its objective.

The bulk of the enemy's speed and assault boats were also destroyed or heavily damaged by naval artillery. Such enemy forces as succeeded in landing were wiped out by troops from all sections of the German forces when they attempted to attack the dock and penetrate into the town.

According to information so far to hand a destroyer, 9 speed boats and 4 torpedo boats of the enemy were destroyed. Apart from heavy losses to enemy left over 100 prisoners in our hands.

On the German side not a single war vessel was lost. No damage of any kind was done to the submarine bases.

When daylight came German torpedo boats encountered a superior formation of British destroyers, which broke off the engagement after having received several hits.

The official German statement sent to Reuters the day after the raid.
(The National Archives)

detachments of the British Navy attempted to enter the Loire estuary. However, they were quickly spotted by the coastal batteries and submitted to intense fire.

Clearly, the situation was back under full German control. It was, in any case, the impression given at the end of the day, and repeated the following day, which was a Sunday. Gathering for their Sunday meal, locals discussed the raid; some had already secretly listened to the BBC report on the wireless, which was banned under the rules of the occupation.

Gradually, life returned to normal. The able-bodied prisoners were transferred to a prison camp in Rennes; at La Baule, the wounded were allowed to recover, with Lieutenant Corran Purdon acting as interpreter with the German medical team.

***

On Monday, March 30, the local press—which was subject to German censorship—announced that "the British raid on St Nazaire has failed."

But that afternoon, as work resumed on the site of the submarine base, another violent explosion shook the port area. One of the delayed-action torpedoes launched by Micky Wynn had just detonated at the Old Entrance, causing an enormous geyser surmounted by a large mushroom cloud.

Thinking a fresh attack had been launched, the Germans start shouting and running in all directions, opening fire on the workers, who fled rather than retaliate and risk retribution.

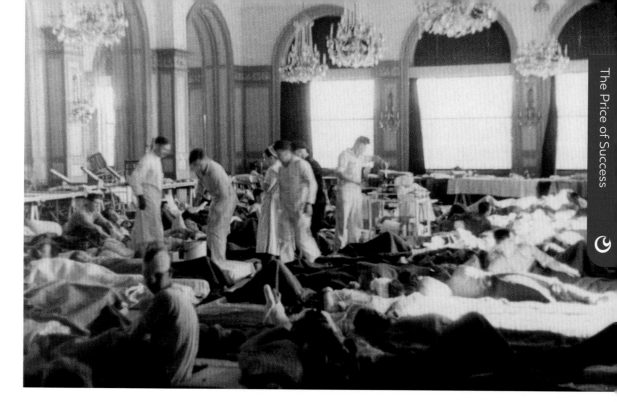

British wounded receive first aid at a hotel in La Baule, converted into a temporary hospital. (St Nazaire Ecomuseum)

APPEL
A LA POPULATION

Les autorités allemandes affirment que des civils français ont participé hier soir à des actes de guerre contre l'armée d'occupation.

Nous ne pouvons pas croire que cela se soit produit.

Nous devons seulement porter immédiatement à la connaissance de nos concitoyens l'avis qui vient de nous être donné :

La population entière sera tenue pour responsable de tout nouvel attentat.

Si les coupables ne sont pas découverts sur le champ, le dixième des habitants du quartier où le fait se sera produit sera fusillé sans jugement sans préjudice de mesures plus générales pouvant frapper l'ensemble de la population.

Ainsi donc tout coup porté à l'armée allemande sera un coup porté à des Français.

Nous faisons à nouveau un appel pressant à la population pour qu'elle conserve son calme et sa dignité.

Saint-Nazaire, le 31 Mars 1942.

P. TOSCER, Maire.

GEORGELIN, GARREC, GAUFFRIAU, GRIMAUD,
adjoints.

The notice posted on the streets of St Nazaire on March 31, signed by the mayor. (St Nazaire Municipal Archives)

St. Nazaire: *The whole glorious story*

DESTROYER HIT DOCK GATES AT 20 KNOTS

Through an inferno of shells like "a ferret diving into a hole"

Exchange reporter with the St. Nazaire Raiding Forces.

THE most daring and most important of combined operational attacks on the enemy so far undertaken has met with splendid success, but the cost has not been light.

Many of the Commando troops who forced home the attack fought on until they were either casualties or taken prisoner.

But they completed one of the finest aggressive operations we have engaged in since the war started.

Naval personnel took the destroyer Campbeltown from England to her destination astride the gates of the big dry-dock at St. Nazaire.

STILL FIRING

They took her with the utmost inevitability, defying U-boats, mines, coastal defences and concentrated harbour fire, and did not stop until they had crashed through the boom defences and charged the dock entrance.

Here the gallant Campbeltown came to her end, while Navy men and Commandos, who had shown the highest courage in manning her in this last historic voyage, still fired her guns.

The bows holding the explosives were ablaze. Only when the flames spread did they run from the decks straight on to the adjacent landing stages which were swept by Nazi fire.

The full extent of their courage was only manifest to the Germans some time later, when the five tons of explosive in the Campbeltown blew the ship and dock entrance and a lot more besides into a tangled, twisted ruin.

LIKE VINDICTIVE

So the destroyer, still so thoroughly American in her lines, found at her end a place in history alongside the Vindictive, block ship of Zeebrugge.

To the Commandos fell the lot of forcing home this attack on an area which has the concentrated defences of a small Portsmouth or a Plymouth. The story of their amazing exploits is one of the most stirring that this country has had during the whole course of the war.

They went ashore in the early hours of the morning, and systematically wrecked harbour installations, lock gates and power houses. They were met by strong opposition, but this they overcame with the utmost determination.

The British naval forces approached St. Nazaire during the course of an R.A.F. bombing attack on the harbour.

I was in a motor gunboat with Commander R. E. D. Ryder and Lieutenant-

➤ BACK PAGE, COL. ONE

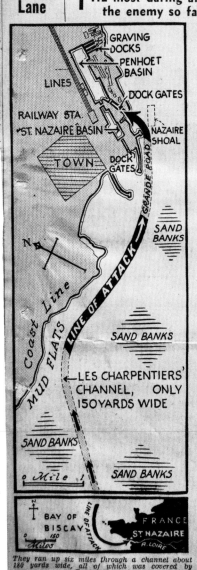

GRAVING DOCKS
PENHOET BASIN
LINES
DOCK GATES
RAILWAY STA
ST. NAZAIRE BASIN
NAZAIRE SHOAL
TOWN
DOCK GATES
GRANDE ROAD
SAND BANKS
N
LINE OF ATTACK
Coast Line
MUD FLATS
SAND BANKS
LES CHARPENTIERS' CHANNEL, ONLY 150 YARDS WIDE
SAND BANKS
o Mile 1
SAND BANKS

BAY OF BISCAY
LINE OF ATTACK
FRANCE
ST NAZAIRE
R. LOIRE
o   150
Miles

They ran up six miles through a channel about 180 yards wide, all of which was covered by German batteries.

In the days that followed, the British newspapers dedicated their front pages to the raid. (The National Archives)

The explosion of the second torpedo, an hour later, ratcheted up the tension another notch; this time the Germans were convinced that it was an act of sabotage perpetrated by French.

The situation had in fact become so confusing that some German troops were yet again firing on men from the Todt Organization, mistaking them for British commandos because of their khaki uniforms. Herbert Sohler himself took several flesh wounds as he rushed to the port from La Baule; the officer accompanying him was also wounded.

The Germans scoured the port and its surroundings. In anger and confusion, they brutalized the St Nazaire locals, shooting and throwing grenades at the slightest suspicious movement. These disorderly reprisals continued until nightfall, resulting in the deaths of between 15 and 25 locals—including a 5-year-old boy struck by two projectiles while he sat with his mother in the kitchen—and wounding nearly thirty.

A little before midnight, the mayor, Pierre Toscer, and four of his deputies were taken by the Feldgendarmerie to the Saint-Louis College, where the offices of the military administration were located. There, the municipal delegation was presented to a staff colonel, who had arrived from Angers that afternoon. Fixing the Frenchmen with an icy glare, the colonel accused the locals of deliberately attacking the Germans. As a result of this insubordination, he continued in a threatening tone, he would shoot one-tenth of the inhabitants of the responsible neighborhood if such an event happened again. And if that was not enough to stamp out the perceived rebellion, he concluded, he would raze the entire city to the ground.

Destroyer Filled With Explosives Shatters St. Nazaire's Lock

From GORDON HOLMAN, Exchange Telegraph Special Correspondent With The Commandos

AT A HOME PORT, Sunday.

THE NAZI-HELD PORT OF ST. NAZAIRE ON THE FRENCH COAST HAS BEEN SMASHED BY THE COMMANDOS, ROYAL NAVY AND R.A.F. IN A RAID WHICH WILL LIVE AS AN EPIC OF BRITISH COURAGE.

The huge dry dock (the only one on the Atlantic coast big enough to hold a German battleship) is blocked by the explosion-twisted remains of a gallant ex-United States destroyer (U.S.S. Buchanan), now H.M.S. Campbeltown.

In many ways the most important of combined operational attacks on the enemy so far undertaken, the raid met with splendid success, but the cost has not been light.

Many of the Commando troops who forced home the attack fought on until they were either casualties or taken prisoner, but they completed one of the finest aggressive operations we have engaged in since the war started.

Naval personnel took the specially prepared destroyer Campbeltown from England to her destination, defying enemy submarines, mines, coastal defences and concentrated harbour fire, and did not stop until they had crashed through the boom

Exclusive News Chronicle picture of Special Service troops who took part in the raid on St. Nazaire on their return to a British port yesterday. In the centre is the officer who led them into action

This picture of Commander R. E. D. Ryder, who commanded the naval forces in the St. Nazaire raid, was taken two weeks ago. Biographies of the men who led the raid are on

The neighborhood in question was the St Nazaire old town. The inhabitants were unceremoniously packed into bunkers for the night. On Tuesday morning, they were transported by bus to a prison camp near Savenay, about 30 kilometers inland. Approximately 1,500 men, women, and children spent three days in unsanitary barracks, guarded by soldiers and dogs.

Upon leaving their homes on the morning of Tuesday, March 31, the Nazairites who had not been rounded up found on the walls of the city the notice addressed to the local population, signed by their mayor and four deputies who had met the Germans:

> The entire population will be held responsible for any new attacks. If the culprits are not identified on the spot, one-tenth of the inhabitants of the district where the event occurred will be shot without judgment, and without prejudice to more general measures that may affect the entire population.

On the other side of the Channel, the tone was rather different. On March 29, Ryder received the following message from Combined Operations Headquarters: "Well done. Magnificent show."

The next day, the British press took up the reins: "Destroyer Hit Dock Gates At 20 Knots," "Lock Out Of Action For Months," and "Commando Raid Was Complete Surprise" were just some of the headlines in the daily newspapers, some of which also carried Ryder's picture or a photo of the commandos smiling during the return trip.

Lieutenant-Commander Herbert Sohler, commander of the 7th U-boat Flotilla, at the funeral of the German troops killed during the raid. (Bundesarchiv)

During the burial of British soldiers at Escoublac cemetery on April 1, 1942, Lieutenant Hopwood, who had disembarked the *Campbeltown* at the head of a protection squad, was greeted by a German officer and chaplain. (Bundesarchiv)

***

On March 31, Field Marshal Gerd von Rundstedt, Oberbefehlshaber West, or Supreme Commander in the West, arrived at St Nazaire, having left his headquarters at Saint-Germain-en-Laye on Hitler's personal orders. Unable to explain how such an significant enemy force could reach the port and land troops without being intercepted by the various air, sea, and land defenses, the Führer demanded the names of all those responsible for this unforgivable humiliation, whom he threatened to bring before a war tribunal.

The next day, Wednesday, April 1 while von Rundstedt continued his investigation at St Nazaire, funerals for the dead on both sides were held at the cemetery of Escoublac, near La Baule. The German authorities invited the British to send a detachment: 20 prisoners attended, bareheaded, in two rows, alongside the soldiers they had been fighting four days earlier.

For a few minutes, the war was forgotten. The Wehrmacht laid a funeral wreath in honor of their enemies killed during the raid, while a platoon of the 280th German Naval Artillery Battalion fired a salute in their honor. Lieutenant Jack Hopwood, the most senior member of the British contingent, was greeted with courtesy and respect by several German officers.

The British commandos who survived the raid did not remain in St Nazaire for very long. As soon as their condition improved, the wounded were transferred to the Saint-Vincent military hospital in Rennes. The able-bodied men were are also sent to Rennes, albeit to a PoW camp.

It was there that Charles Newman was visited by a German officer, sent by the commander of the *Jaguar*. The commander, explained the messenger, wished to draw the attention of the British to the heroic behavior of one of their non-commissioned officers

He won V.C. at St. Nazaire

Commander R. E. Dudley Ryder, R.N., leaving Buckingham Palace with his wife, after he had received from the King the V.C. won by him in the attack on St. Nazaire, when he led a force of unprotected ships against the heavily defended port.

Commander Ryder, photographed here alongside his wife, was decorated with the Victoria Cross by King George VI for successfully leading the British flotilla at St Nazaire. (The National Archives)

serving on board one of the motorboats captured during the fight; behavior, he said, that was deserving of "the highest honor." Newman did not yet know that the man in question was Sergeant Tom Durrant, who had continued firing on Lieutenant Paul's torpedo boat, until his bullet-riddled body had collapsed onto the blood-soaked deck.

As a result of this astonishing intervention, the valiant NCO was posthumously awarded the Victoria Cross, the highest British military honor. Even more extraordinary was that the honor was granted on the recommendation of an enemy officer.

After Rennes, the prisoners were split up and sent to various camps in Germany. Their fighting spirit had not been blunted, and many attempted to break out of the PoW camps. Some, like Micky Wynn, Corran Purdon, and Michael Burn were punished for their escape attempts with a stint at the infamous fortress of Colditz, in Saxony.

All in all, only five commandos who took part in Operation *Chariot* managed to comply with the order given by Newman in the St Nazaire mousetrap: get to Gibraltar. Hidden in basements, they fled the city under the cover of darkness and into the countryside. The "final five" were Corporal Douglas, Private Robert Sims, and Private Harding, all of Warrant Officer Haines's assault group; Private Howarth, from Lieutenant Roderick's assault group; and Corporal George Wheeler, a member of Lieutenant Walton's demolition team. Once back in Britain, the five commandos rejoined their units and continued serving until the end of the war.

For the British, the human toll of *Chariot* was heavy. Of the 611 men engaged, 169 were killed or posted missing, and 232 captured, including nearly 100 wounded. The Royal Navy lost 189: 103 killed, and 86 captured. As for the commandos, 66 were killed, and 146 captured.

Despite these significant losses, the operation was still considered a success. Its main objective, the neutralization of the Joubert lock, had been achieved. The *Campbeltown* explosion did so much damage to the lock that it was out of action for rest of the war. As for the *Tirpitz*, the ultimate motivation for Operation *Chariot*, it never entered the Atlantic. The German dreadnaught suffered the same fate as its sister ship, the *Bismarck*: on November 12, 1944, it was sunk by RAF bombers in a Norwegian fjord.

But while the performance of the *Campbeltown* and the commandos on board was deemed a success, the same could not be said of the motorboat flotilla. They may have been fast, but the wooden motor launches were fragile and insufficiently armed, and were no match for the German coastal batteries. [direct quotation needed - "Most were destroyed for the main reason that they just were not made for it. They were made to burn. It was not really

On August 2, 1947, the "Charioteers" returned to St Nazaire for the first time since the raid. Charles Newman and Robert Ryder lead their men over the swing bridge, watched by local residents. (National Archives)

Former commando Lieutenant Bill "Tiger" Watson on the 71st anniversary of the raid, March 28, 2013. (J.-C. Stasi)

the fault of the Royal Navy; the rule was to use what materials were available, and the raid on St Nazaire stuck to that rule,"] reasoned Robert Ryder after the war, with his customary bluntness.

The vulnerability of the motorboats inevitably brought another issue to light: that of the diversionary air raid. It took place, of course, but all agreed that it was too short and not intense enough. About 60 aircraft were engaged, but no more than six actually dropped their bombs. "It wasn't a complete surprise, mainly because of the noise from the motor launches' engines, audible in calm weather for up to three miles, and because of the bombers' inability to locate their targets due to bad weather," noted a British report dated April 13, 1942. Charles Newman's official statement, made when he returned from captivity in 1945, noted that all the fire he had seen during the raid had been horizontal—aimed at the raiders.

On the German side, Lieutenant Mecke, commander of the 22nd Naval Flak Brigade, admitted in a report requested by Hitler that had the Royal Air Force continued its bombing, the British vessels would probably have reached St Nazaire without being spotted.

The majority of the motorboats were unable to land their commandos, and many of the other objectives were not achieved either. Nowhere was this truer than at the New Entrance, where the swing bridge and locks remained perfectly intact, allowing the submarine base to remain in service for the remainder of the war.

The Joubert lock after the war. It only returned to service in 1947. (Hubert Chemereau)

Stephen Barney, action helmsman on the *Atherstone*, on the beach of St Nazaire during the 71st anniversary of the raid, March 28, 2013. Barney died on September 23, 2017 aged 95, one of the last survivors of Operation *Chariot*. (J.-C. Stasi)

| Afterword

Though it is generally agreed today that the German high command had no plans to deploy the *Tirpitz* following the departure of the *Scharnhorst*, *Gneisenau*, and heavy cruiser *Prinz Eugen* from Brest in February 1942, at the time, Operation *Chariot* was fully justified.

Following the raid on St Nazaire, Hitler withdrew troops from the Eastern Front to reinforce his defenses in the West.

Finally, we cannot fully appreciate the effect of Operation *Chariot* without taking into account the psychological impact it had on the parties involved. If the raid did have an effect on people's spirits both in occupied Europe and in Germany, it was because it created a small but significant chink in the previously invulnerable veneer of the Nazi war machine.

In his report, Newman made the point that at the time of the raid, England had been on the defensive since Dunkirk. He noted that the raid on St Nazaire would be remembered as the first offensive action against the enemy in Europe, and that it had affected the country's outlook, encouraging Britain to look ahead, not back to the dark days of 1940.

Two years later, on August, 1947, French politician and Prime Minister of the Fourth Republic, Paul Ramadier, expanded the scope of Newman's judgment, welcoming the survivors of *Chariot* back to St Nazaire, on their first visit since the raid. "You were the first to bring us hope. Your magnificent night was the dawn of our liberation!" he declared with enthusiasm as the British—Newman and Ryder at their head—stood in the harbor they had assaulted five years earlier.

Operation *Chariot* resulted in 74 decorations and 51 citations for its participants. Five Victoria Crosses, Britain's highest award for bravery, were awarded to Lieutenant-Colonel Charles Newman, commander of the ground forces; Commander Robert Ryder, commander of the naval component; Lieutenant-Commander Sam Beattie, commander of the *Campbeltown*; and posthumously to Sergeant Thomas Durrant, and Able Seaman William Savage.

After the war, Lieutenant Mecke, whose 22nd Naval Flak Brigade gave the Charioteers so much trouble, wrote the following of his adversaries:

> Whatever the strategic considerations, this raid, whose chances of success were only about one in nine, was conducted with great care and courage. Those who achieved it deserve not only the recognition of their compatriots, but also the respect of their former enemies, who recognize the bravery that had to be shown in its execution.

More ominously, British commando raids were becoming so effective that by October 1942 Adolf Hitler issued the infamous "Commando Order," whereby all captured commandos were to be executed.

| Sources

Books

Batteson, Ralph. *St. Nazaire to Shepperton: A Sailor's Odyssey* (Highedge Historical Society 1996)

Brauer, Luc and Petitjean, Bernard. *Raid sur Saint-Nazaire!: 28 Mars 1942: Opération Chariot* (2003)

Brauer, Luc. *Le base sous-marine de La Rochelle* (2018)

Burn, Michael. *Turned Towards the Sun: An Autobiography* (Michael Russell Publishing Ltd., Norwich 2003)

Dorrian, James G. *Storming St. Nazaire* (Naval Institute Press, Annapolis 1998)

Flamond, Roger. *L'inconnu du French Squadron* (1983)

Forbes, Charles M. *The attack on St Nazaire, 1942* (*London Gazette*, London 1942)

Lucas Phillips, C. E. *The Greatest Raid of All* (Pan, London 2000)

Lyman, Robert. *Into the Jaws of Death: The True Story of the Legendary Raid on Saint-Nazaire* (Quercus, London 2014)

Mason David. *Raid on St. Nazaire* (Hazell Watson, UK ed. 1970)

Masson, Philippe. *La bataille de l'Atlantique* (FeniXX réédition numérique (Tallandier) 1997)

Purdon, Corran. *List the Bugle: Reminiscences of an Irish Soldier* (Greystone Books, Vancouver 1993)

Stanley, Peter. *Commando to Colditz: Micky Burn's Journey to the Far Side of Tears, Remembering the Raid on St Nazaire* (Pier 9, Murdoch Books, Amazon 2009)

Vérine, Yann. *Les commandos par mer de la Deuxième Guerre mondiale* (2018)

Periodicals

"Débarquement à Saint-Nazaire," colonel Rémy, revue *Historama*, no. 303

Le Populaire

"Les Bretons et l'opération Chariot," Hubert Chemereau, revue *ArMen*, no. 187

"Les sous-mariniers allemandes," *Gazette des uniformes*, hors-série no. 5

Ouest-France

Presse Océan

"Raid sur Saint-Nazaire," Ronald Mc Nair, revue *39–45 magazine*, no. 65

Other

Bundesarchiv

Coastal Forces Veterans: http://cfv.org.uk/research/history/article/st-nazaire-the-greatest-raid

Commando Veterans' Association: www.commandoveterans.org

Imperial War Museum

Interviews with Stephen Barney (March 2013), Bill "Tiger" Watson (March 2013), Corran Purdon (May 2013)

Operation Chariot: www.jamesgdorrian.com

St Nazaire Society: www.stnazairesociety.org

The National Archives

| Index